THE SCHOOL LEADER'S GUIDE TO SEND

Other titles from Bloomsbury Education

SEND Strategies for the Primary Years: Practical ideas and expert advice to use pre-diagnosis by Georgina Durrant

SEND Strategies for the Secondary Years: Practical ideas and expert advice to support and understand young people by Georgina Durrant

The Inclusive Classroom: A new approach to differentiation by Daniel Sobel and Sara Alston

The Strategic SENCo: How to lead whole school inclusion with vision and purpose by Kenny Wheeler

The Ultimate Guide to Adaptive Teaching: Confidently meeting the needs of every learner by Sue Cowley

Other titles by the same author

Starting Out as a Primary SENCo: Finding your first post, the first year and beyond by Lynn How

Further titles from Bloomsbury Education are available at:
www.bloomsbury.com/uk/education

THE SCHOOL LEADER'S GUIDE TO SEND

Inclusive leadership in practice

LYNN HOW

BLOOMSBURY EDUCATION
LONDON OXFORD NEW YORK NEW DELHI SYDNEY

BLOOMSBURY EDUCATION
Bloomsbury Publishing Plc
50 Bedford Square, London WC1B 3DP, UK
Bloomsbury Publishing Ireland Limited
29 Earlsfort Terrace, Dublin 2, D02 AY28, Ireland

First published in Great Britain, 2026 by Bloomsbury Publishing Plc
This edition published in Great Britain, 2026 by Bloomsbury Publishing Plc

A catalogue record for this book is available from the British Library

ISBN: PB: 978-1-80199-769-0; eBook: 978-1-80199-770-6

2 4 6 8 10 9 7 5 3 1 (paperback)

Cover design by James Fraser

Typeset by Lumina Datamatics Ltd

Printed and bound in Great Britain by TJ Books, Padstow, Cornwall

To find out more about our authors and books visit www.bloomsbury.com and sign up for our newsletters
For product safety related questions contact productsafety@bloomsbury.com

Contents

Foreword

Want to see inclusion? Start here.

How timely, to read a practical book for teachers when SEND reform is once again part of the national conversation. Lynn How brings a rare dual perspective: the strategic eye of a school leader and the practical expertise of an experienced SENDCo (in that order). This is a guide rooted in lived experience, research and usable tools for busy teachers and leaders.

Notice who is noticed

If you want to know what a school's culture is really like, don't start with its prospectus. Don't start with its values displayed on reception walls. Stand in a corridor during lesson changeover. Sit at the back of a classroom. Watch how the adults speak to the pupils, especially the ones who are 'late again'. Notice those who are dysregulated or anxious, or are quietly masking everything behind perfect classroom compliance. In those small moments, you will see what the school truly believes about inclusion. Not what it says it believes, but what it does when the day becomes busy, when staff are tired, when the timetable is stretched, or when the local authority has not called back to complete the assessment that should have happened months ago. After 35 years in education, I have watched SEND move from the margins of school improvement to the centre of almost every serious conversation about standards, attendance, behaviour, safeguarding, curriculum and wellbeing. SEND needs and challenges have always been there, of course. Young people have not suddenly become complex, as some might argue. What has changed is our understanding of SEND, our literacy and knowledge, our expertise in identification and needs, our expectations, and, sadly, the scale of unmet need.

The most revealing leadership test

Without doubt, one of the greatest tests of school leadership is how a school supports the pupils who do not fit neatly into its systems. It is easy to write an inclusion policy. It is much harder to build a school where inclusion survives Monday morning. Creating routines, training, communication and accountability is even tougher. Inclusion cannot depend on the goodwill of one exhausted SENDCo, one brilliant teaching assistant, or one teacher who 'just gets it'. I have worked with school leaders across the country who are trying to hold two truths at once. First, not every child who worries needs a diagnosis. Second, every young person who is struggling deserves support. The danger in the current debate is that we allow these two truths to be set against each other. They are not opposites. There is a world of difference between normalising everyday nerves and dismissing a young person who is living in a state of hypervigilance. There is a difference between encouraging resilience and ignoring trauma. There is a difference between challenging low expectations and pretending that barriers do not exist. This is where school leadership matters, particularly the excellent leadership of SEND.

The provision crisis

When I published my book, *Just Great Teaching*, in 2019, I was already seeing evidence of a deepening SEND crisis. Teachers were routinely describing rising numbers of young people presenting with anxiety, ADHD, autism traits, sensory processing difficulties, emotionally based school avoidance and wider mental health needs. At the same time, external services were feeling overwhelmed. Waiting lists were long, and CAMHS teams were stretched. Countless families found themselves fighting for provision rather than being guided towards it. The only thing that's changed since publication is that all of these issues have got worse! This is not simply a misdiagnosis problem. It is a provision crisis. In some classrooms, teachers are doing extraordinary work with very little. They are adapting explanations, adjusting seating plans, pre-teaching vocabulary, building emotional literacy, managing sensory needs, contacting families, chasing referrals, and trying to protect learning for everyone else in the room. They are doing this while also being told to raise attainment, improve attendance, close gaps, reduce exclusions and maintain their own wellbeing. No wonder some schools feel as if they are permanently firefighting. Inclusion cannot depend on individual heroism or on one school working alone. Effective inclusion provision must become an inherent part of our education and welfare system.

Small routines, big signals

The strongest inclusive schools I have visited did not always have the most money, although funding matters enormously. They do not always have perfect buildings, instant access to specialists, or limitless staffing. What they do have is clarity. They know what every classroom should offer before any additional label, referral or plan is written. They know what good universal provision looks like. They know how staff should respond when a child is dysregulated. They know when to seek specialist support. They know how to work with families without becoming defensive. They know that behaviour is communication, but they also know that adults need systems, training and time if they are to respond well. Most importantly, they do *not* leave SEND to the SENDCo. The SENDCo is not a paperwork machine. They are a strategic leader, and if a school's SEND lead has no time, no authority and no meaningful place in senior decision-making, then inclusion will always be fragile. It may survive on relationships, but it will not be sustained by the organisation. I have learned, sometimes the hard way, that the most inclusive leadership decisions are often the least glamorous: protected time for staff to meet; a sharper transition process; a better seating plan; a simpler pupil profile; more training for support staff; a behaviour policy that understands trauma and diversity; a senior team that listens carefully before it judges quickly. These decisions rarely make the headlines, but they do change lives.

The reform moment

The current SEND reform debate in England places greater emphasis on mainstream inclusion, early support, tiered provision and stronger expectations for all schools. In principle, few teachers would argue with this ambition. Our young people should receive help earlier. Families should not have to battle for every adjustment. Teachers should not have to wait years for specialist advice before doing the right thing. But reform will fail if it becomes another set of expectations placed on schools without the workforce, funding and specialist capacity to deliver it. Inclusion cannot be mandated into existence. It has to be taught, led and revisited. And this is why this book matters. *The School Leader's Guide to SEND* is a timely and practical contribution to a national challenge that is not going away. Written by an experienced teacher and SEND expert, Lynn How understands the reality of SEND leadership: the competing pressures, the paperwork, the relationships, the frustrations, and the moral purpose that keeps people going. This book does not treat inclusion as a slogan. It treats it as a daily practice. It helps leaders think carefully about culture, universal provision, SENDCo leadership, support staff, families, inspection, accountability and the many decisions that shape a child's experience of school. Every school leader is now, whether they've planned to be or not, a leader of SEND. The question is not whether the school should be inclusive. The question is whether leaders know how to make inclusion coherent, sustainable and visible in the ordinary life of the school. In the book, Lynn shows us how, making it an important publication for anyone working with young people across the UK.

Ross Morrison McGill
Former school leader, bestselling author and founder of @TeacherToolkit.

Introduction

Hello, and thank you for choosing this book!

I'm excited to have the opportunity to share my insights and experiences to help you support Special Educational Needs and Disabilities (SEND) education within your school. Every school leader plays a crucial role in the development and success of students with SEND. Just as the SEND Code of Practice states, *every teacher is a teacher of SEND* (Department for Education and Department of Health, 2015). By extension, every school leader is a leader of SEND. Happily, through talking extensively to colleagues and others in my online and personal networks, it's clear that most school leaders are overwhelmingly keen to improve inclusion within their settings.

I *love* being a SENDCo and everything SEND-related. My first book, *Starting Out as a Primary SENCo*, came together so naturally I felt as if it just flowed straight out of my head and onto the page – I'm hoping this one will be the same!

Unlike many SENDCos, I came into the profession from a different angle. From what I've seen, most SENDCos step up from class teacher, and the role is usually their first chance to lead a whole-school area. My path was different: I'd been an assistant head for a decade and had completed both my MA and NPQH before I even started as a SENDCo. That background gave me valuable insight into whole-school leadership and a strong grasp of the bigger picture of running a school.

As SENDCos, it's easy to develop 'tunnel vision'. We're so passionate about our area (and often so frustrated by the state of it), that we sometimes forget there are other students and priorities in a school too! But the mantra '*what's good for students with SEND is good for everyone*' helps bring us back to some common ground. It reminds us that inclusive practice doesn't sit in a silo; it lifts the whole school.

How will this book help you?

The aim of this book is to offer an accessible, time-efficient read for busy school leaders, covering not only the essentials but also the more complex and topical aspects of SEND in modern schools. Everything I've written is rooted in a mixture of my own experience (including working with eight headteachers so far — some of whom taught me how *not* to do it), my academic research, and the extensive insights and anecdotes shared across my online networks of SENDCos.

My goal is to provide practical, manageable solutions but they aren't set in stone. There's no single 'correct' way to implement best practice. As with any professional advice, take what is useful and relevant to your context, and feel entirely free to adapt (or ignore!) the rest.

You'll find discussions on:

- unpicking the challenges senior leaders face in inclusion and supporting students with SEND
- understanding and amplifying pupil voice so pupils can articulate what they need to succeed
- empathising with the realities of 'wearing so many hats' as a headteacher, and balancing SEND with whole-school priorities
- exploring the barriers leaders encounter in their own continuing professional development (CPD) around SEND, from constraints to stretched resources
- reflecting on the national picture for SEND students in mainstream settings and considering when a specialist setting might be more appropriate
- securing further funding and navigating the complexities around it
- building strong, trusting relationships with parents, staff, governors and students to strengthen inclusion
- serving the wider community in ways that support inclusion, build relationships and promote progress for key groups
- showcasing case studies of schools doing exceptional work
- highlighting the importance of the SENDCo and the value of a strong senior leader–SENDCo partnership
- sharing honest insight into what SENDCos think about senior leaders (and believe me, they aren't shy about it!)
- ... and plenty more!

I'm guessing that if you've chosen to read this book, you're already committed to inclusion and looking to build on what's already working well in your school, which is amazing! I would ask, though, that if you know any school leaders who aren't especially inclusive, you consider passing this book on once you've finished it. I wrote it not only for the school leaders who *want* to engage with SEND, but also for the ones who would never buy this book in a million years!

Whatever your reason for picking it up, thank you. I hope you find it genuinely useful.

Companion website

The book has a companion website at bloomsbury.pub/leaders-guide-send, where you will find extra resources, templates and guidance.

Part 1

Knowledge and understanding of SEND

1 Barriers to school leaders' SEND knowledge and understanding

With the best will in the world, it's impossible to do everything we set out to in a day, a week, a year, or even a lifetime. So as you read this section, please be kind to yourself. There are myriad reasons why school leaders aren't as clued up on SEND as they'd like to be. In a profession where we tend to self-flagellate over just about everything, don't add this to your list. This section highlights some common barriers school leaders face when trying to understand and embed inclusive practice in their schools.

Ah, where to start with the barriers school leaders face when trying to create an inclusive environment? It can feel like a perpetual game of Whack-a-Mole – just as you deal with one issue, another pops up. In this section, I outline some barriers that are frequently mentioned.

Of course, your school will have its own nuances rooted in your context, history and demographics, but many challenges are common across settings. Here's a brief overview of some that come to mind – see if you can get a full house on Barrier Bingo as you read this list!

Funding (or the lack of it)

Let's start with the big one. Meeting the individual needs of students with SEND is difficult when you're constantly fighting for resources. Specialist staff, appropriate interventions and even accessible classrooms don't just magically appear – they cost money.

The mythical £6,000 per-student notional budget (which is not a legally enforceable funding assumption) was set over a decade ago, and, oddly enough, while inflation and the cost of living have risen, the budget has not. That shortfall is just one drop in a much wider sea of financial pressures. Put simply, it's not getting any easier.

Staffing

Even if you manage to juggle the finances, securing the right staff to support complex needs is a major hurdle. Recruiting highly skilled SENDCos, learning support assistants (LSAs) or external specialists (speech and language therapists, occupational therapists, etc.) is no mean feat, especially when there are national shortages across these professions.

Although therapeutic input should be funded by the local authority (LA) when provision is specified in an Education, Health and Care Plan (EHCP), getting that specification agreed is becoming increasingly challenging. Schools now often have to buy in their own therapists. With such high need and limited health service capacity, this is both widely necessary and, frankly, a luxury.

Even when you do find the right people, getting them into the right roles – and keeping them there – can feel like a logistical nightmare. Of course, you can't actually stop people from moving on, but creating a culture where the grass doesn't look greener elsewhere goes a long way. This doesn't have to be expensive; it's more about mindset and culture (more on that later).

Ongoing training

Ongoing training is another major challenge. Staff need the knowledge and strategies to support students well, but leaders are already spinning a hundred other plates. There simply aren't enough INSET days (known in my house as 'bug days' because my son once thought they were insect days and wanted to know why his sister got a bug day and he didn't!) to cover everything. As you pay support staff by the hour, you need to consider the best use of their time as well. When so much energy goes into firefighting, strategic CPD, especially for LSAs, is often squeezed out.

Time constraints

The SEND Code of Practice is a genuinely useful document... if you ever get the time to implement it properly! School leaders are stretched between meeting students' needs, keeping on top of endless admin and still finding space to lead teaching and learning – and that's before you even attempt to maintain a personal life or a sense of humour.

I've certainly felt a marked shift since the curriculum ramp-up in 2014, and another sharp one after the post-COVID surge in SEND demand. It's no wonder that time – or the lack of it – remains one of the biggest obstacles to embedding inclusive practice.

External pressures

Governors and trustees are often well-meaning but their understanding of SEND – and of their role within it – can vary widely. If you're working with a supportive, knowledgeable, friendly governing body, you're doing well. In my experience, they can sometimes be more concerned with performance data and academic results than inclusion. If they're also a parent at the school, it's not uncommon for their own child's needs to dominate their perspective.

It's a balancing act: demonstrating progress and maintaining standards while also supporting students who don't always fit neatly into the 'expected progress' narrative. Ofsted inspections create a lot of anxiety. There is, unfortunately, still a judgment at the end of it, leaving leaders up and down the country wondering whether anything has been learned in the wake of events over the past few years.

At the time of writing, the new framework places a strong emphasis on inclusion, student voice and parental engagement – all positive steps in principle. However, SENDCos in my network report that, without any increase in release time or resources to support this shift, their stress levels have risen sharply.

Leaders are trying to meet Ofsted requirements while also working towards meaningful, student-centred inclusion. But the pressure to secure a favourable Ofsted rating can sometimes result in a tokenistic approach to inclusion rather than the deep, sustainable change students actually need.

Lack of specialist provision

For students with complex SEND needs, mainstream schools aren't always the most appropriate setting. Yet here they are, because there simply aren't enough specialist placements available. This creates a huge barrier for leaders who are trying to adapt a mainstream environment to meet needs that exceed what the school can realistically offer. It's frustrating and often heart-wrenching to know that some students could thrive in a specialist environment that just isn't available.

I've heard recently that many schools previously categorised as supporting pupils with moderate learning difficulties (MLD) are now reclassifying as settings for severe learning difficulties (SLD). This may help pupils with SLD who are currently 'stuck' in mainstream and not having their needs fully met. I'm also hearing that some specialist providers are shifting their intake to Year 3 and above. Inevitably, this has a knock-on effect for primary schools, particularly given the rising levels of need in the Early Years Foundation Stage (EYFS) and Key Stage 1.

Parental expectations

Parents, understandably, want the very best for their children, and many have very clear (and sometimes very fixed) views about what that should look like. Balancing those expectations with the realistic limits of what a mainstream school can offer is tricky – to put it mildly. You may find yourself having difficult conversations explaining, often repeatedly, that a school can't meet every need perfectly, however hard it tries. This challenge is compounded by the temptation to gloss over gaps in provision rather than name them openly, a response that's closely linked with wider systemic issues. Honesty's harder in the moment, but more sustainable in the long run.

Policy and legislation

Government policy can be a double-edged sword. Frameworks such as the Children and Families Act, the SEND Code of Practice and the Wellbeing Guidance are incredibly valuable – on paper. Too often, national policy sets expectations without fully supporting schools to meet them.

Maintaining staff wellbeing

An inclusive environment doesn't just care for its students – it cares for its staff. Sustaining an 'anti-burnout establishment' matters for everyone: teachers, LSAs and leaders alike. The pressures of supporting students with SEND within a stretched system makes staff wellbeing an essential leadership priority, not an optional one. Keeping morale and functionality intact is even more important when expectations are high and resources are limited.

School leaders' understanding of SEND

Some school leaders have a fairly limited understanding of the SENDCo's role and the complexities involved in supporting students with SEND. The *National SENDCo Workforce Survey* (Bath Spa, 2021), found that only 53 per cent of primary SENDCos and just 25 per cent of secondary SENDCos felt their role was fully understood by their senior leadership teams (SLT).

So, while this book may involve a certain amount of preaching to the converted, it's worth acknowledging that, in some settings, this lack of understanding stretches SENDCos across too many responsibilities, reduces the time allocated to the role and results in insufficient support for SEND-specific initiatives. Because of current pressures, school leaders may understandably focus on immediate academic outcomes at the expense of long-term SENDCo SEND strategies, underestimating the time, training and resources required across the whole staff. But without a clear, strategic grasp of SEND, SLTs will struggle to deliver whole-school, inclusive education.

Minimum and maximum offers in mainstream education

So, what can (and should) mainstream schools be offering? In an ideal world, every child would receive the highest-quality education in an inclusive, well-resourced setting. In reality, mainstream schools are asked to go above and beyond their capacity while still operating within the confines of 'best endeavours', as set out in Section 66 of the Children and Families Act (2014):

> *If a registered pupil or a student at a school or other institution has special educational needs, the appropriate authority must, in exercising its functions in relation to the school or other institution, use its best endeavours to secure that the special educational provision called for by the pupil's or student's special educational needs is made.*
>
> (Excerpt from the Children and Families Act 2014, legislation.gov.uk).

This offer isn't just about legal compliance; it's about meeting needs, supporting personal growth and helping each student achieve their full potential. This section of the book, then, explores the current expectations for mainstream schools, focusing on universal provision (best-quality teaching for all students) and tiered support (targeted and adapted interventions for learners requiring additional help).

At its heart, this is about building a school culture where excellent teaching is embedded throughout, benefiting all learners, including those with SEND. Of course, many schools are struggling to offer the basics comfortably, let alone provide a gold-standard offer. It's a massive grey area and my aim is to help your SLT understand both the bare minimum and the realistic upper limits of what you can provide. At the other end of the spectrum, I also want to help you spot when your LA might be taking the proverbial 'biscuit' (feel free to substitute a stronger word!).

Before you dive into the reflection questions...

You might not have all the answers yet, and that's absolutely fine. This isn't about catching you out. It's an opportunity to pause, reflect and take stock of your current practice. Some questions may feel uncomfortable or reveal areas for development, but they're intended as useful touchpoints you can revisit over time. Think of them less as a checklist and more as markers of progress as your SEND provision evolves.

Reflection questions

- Do budget constraints affect your ability to implement effective SEND provision? What creative solutions have you found, if any, to help with this?
- Have you faced difficulties recruiting or retaining staff with the skills needed to support SEND students?
- How do you ensure the right people are in place, and what could improve things in your setting?
- How do you manage your staff's ongoing SEND training needs?
- Are there knowledge or practice gaps that still need attention, and what methods (such as internal webinars) might help?

- With so many responsibilities on your plate, how do you prioritise SEND within your school's wider agenda? Are there areas where more time could be given to inclusive practices? If so, how might you reallocate resources?
- Do you experience tension between focusing on inclusion and meeting performance metrics set by Ofsted or your governing body? How do you balance inclusive practice with external expectations?
- Do you have students in your school whose needs can't be fully met in a mainstream setting? How do you navigate that, and what support (if any) do you receive from your LA or specialist provisions?
- How do you manage conversations with parents when their expectations exceed what your school can realistically offer? Have you encountered challenges in maintaining transparency and trust?
- How do current government policies and legislation impact your ability to support SEND students? Do you feel schools are given enough support to meet these requirements?
- What steps are you taking to ensure that your staff, especially those supporting SEND students, aren't overworked or burnt out?
- How do you look after your own wellbeing as a school leader?
- Do you feel your SLT has a strong grasp of the complexities involved in supporting SEND students? If not, what might help deepen their understanding?

2 The foundations of an inclusive school

The minimum offer for students with SEND isn't just about individual interventions; it's about building a whole-school culture where inclusive practice is woven into everything you do. Inclusion doesn't happen overnight. It's a continuous, evolving process that relies on commitment from every member of the school community. Whether you're a classroom teacher, school leader or support staff, genuinely inclusive education means ensuring all students, but particularly those with SEND, have access to the support they need to thrive.

Embedding inclusion across a whole school is inherently challenging, especially if you've inherited a setting where it hasn't been a priority before. But it is possible, and it starts with strong foundations. Here are four essential strategies to ensure inclusion isn't just a policy statement but runs through your school like words through a stick of rock.

Whole-school training: setting the tone for inclusion

One of the first steps towards an inclusive culture is making sure everyone is on the same page. Without whole-school training, inclusion is left to individual interpretation, which inevitably leads to inconsistencies. Staff bring a wide range of experiences, strengths and assumptions, and it takes a collective approach to shape these into coherent whole-school practice.

A strong training programme goes beyond SENDCo-led briefings and should be embedded throughout the professional development cycle, touching every area of school life. Once established, a robust induction package ensures that new staff – including temporary and supply teachers – are brought into the culture straight away.

Staff need to understand not only what SEND looks like, but how to adapt their practice. Everyone should feel confident using adaptive teaching strategies, supporting students with specific needs and addressing common challenges such as emotional dysregulation or sensory sensitivities. Whole-school training should also highlight strategies that benefit everyone (e.g. retrieval practice, scaffolding and Universal Design for Learning (UDL)). Identify which staff members need the most support and use this as a baseline to pitch whole-school training.

Top Tip

Don't limit CPD to SEND-specific content. Broader skills (such as trauma-informed practice, mental health first aid or effective de-escalation) benefit all students and help staff feel more capable and supported.

Remember to revisit, revisit, revisit. The number of initiatives I was absolutely convinced were happening 'regularly', only to find out they had quietly disappeared, is somewhat depressing. I learned the hard way that even when staff are trained, you can't assume the work will continue by itself. Follow-up is essential, and something as central as inclusion deserves sustained focus, discussion and reinforcement.

Collaboration and communication

Working together is essential for supporting learners because it helps everyone understand and meet students' needs. When communication is open and consistent, it creates a more inclusive and supportive learning environment for everyone involved.

One of the trickiest parts of SEND work is the sheer number of people involved. It's rarely just the class teacher: you've got LSAs, speech and language therapists, educational psychologists (EPs) and sometimes medical professionals all playing their part; assuming you can actually get them through the door in the first place. Add in parents, who are often the best experts on their own children but may also bring their own pressures and anxieties. Many appreciate having a single key person who can act as a bridge between home and school, to keep communication timely and straightforward. More communication usually means fewer problems escalate. Prevention is always better than cure, though sometimes a little last-minute damage control is unavoidable. We're only human.

To work well together, everyone needs to communicate openly and regularly. That means talking honestly about what's going well, what isn't, and how to adjust when things don't go to plan – which they often won't.

Put simple systems in place to make this easier, such as regular review meetings, brief update channels (like a shared online folder or document) and a clear point of contact – often the SENDCo – for any questions or concerns. Set key dates at the start of the year.

Top Tip

Collaboration doesn't have to involve endless meetings. Use technology to streamline communication – quick emails, shared documents, short updates. The goal is to spend more time supporting students, not drowning in paperwork.

The SENDCo as a leader: more than just paperwork

SENDCos will tell you the role can feel like spinning a dozen plates at once. But at its core, being a SENDCo is a leadership role that requires strategic thinking, clarity of vision and the ability to bring others along with you. It's about setting the tone for inclusion across the school (with SLT), leading training, coordinating provision, and working alongside families and external agencies to secure the support students need. Whether we actually get five quiet minutes in between bouts of firefighting to think strategically is another matter entirely.

An effective SENDCo occupies a genuinely multifaceted position. Yes, the paperwork matters – annual reviews, EHCP processes and the endless documentation that sits behind SEND provision – but that's only one part of it. The SENDCo is also a senior voice at the decision-making table, advocating for students in everything from curriculum design to timetabling, staffing, transitions and behaviour systems. Inclusion should shape every layer of school life, and the SENDCo plays a central role in making that happen.

To lead well, SENDCos need time, training and influence. They should have access to high-quality professional development not only in SEND but in leadership too, because much of the role involves coaching, guiding and supporting colleagues to adopt inclusive practices.

Top Tip

Give your SENDCo the time their role requires. Without protected time, the demands of the job become overwhelming, and burnout isn't far behind.

Creating an inclusive culture

An inclusive culture isn't something you can label, it's something you feel. It's in the way staff greet students in the morning, the warmth of the interactions you witness, and the strength of the school's ethos. I'm a spiritual soul, and I'd go as far as to say that in the schools that do inclusion well, there's a calming energy you can sense instantly. I love noticing whether my first impression matches what I observe throughout the day and more often than not, it does.

This culture starts with leadership. Senior leaders set the tone: Are they modelling inclusive attitudes? Are they celebrating diversity? Do they make inclusion a standing agenda item rather than a once-a-term afterthought? Crucially, do they hold everyone to account for upholding these values? But inclusive culture doesn't just trickle down, it also grows up. Everyone should *feel ownership* of inclusion. That means empowering teachers to adapt lessons, giving LSAs the skills they need, and helping students learn how to support and understand one another. Inclusion isn't the SENDCo's responsibility alone; it's a shared commitment across the entire school.

Top Tip

Involve students in shaping the culture. Whether through student councils, peer mentors, targeted groups or reflective Personal, Social, Health and Education (PSHE) sessions, give students real opportunities to contribute to and discuss inclusion. The more ownership they feel and the more diverse the voices represented, the stronger and more authentic your school culture becomes.

Reflection questions

- How does your current professional development programme help all staff understand and use inclusive practices? What can you do to make sure inclusion is regularly reviewed and remains a priority in every department?
- Think about the communication systems your school uses. How well do they keep key staff and parents informed?

- Are there ways to use technology more effectively to make updates and feedback easier?
- Does your SENDCo have enough time, resources and authority to lead inclusion well in your school?
- How could the leadership team better support the SENDCo?
- How would you describe your school's current culture of inclusion? Can students, staff and leaders work together to shape and improve this culture?
- What quick changes could help build a more inclusive environment across the school?

3 Universal provision

A mainstream school's minimum offer begins with making sure every student benefits from the universal provision of Tier 1 teaching. It's the foundation on which all further support is built. The goal is to create a classroom where every student in the class can thrive. When schools achieve this it's a joy to behold, but it often takes only a few extra or unexpected elements to tip the balance back towards classroom chaos. The caveat here is that I appreciate that there are also children in our mainstream classes who would be more suited to a specialist environment.

I should add here that, when asked by SENDCos what my top whole-school priority is, this is number one. When universal provision is effectively embedded, it prevents many issues from arising in the first place, leaving staff able to focus on more strategic thinking (or even teaching) and less day-to-day firefighting.

Tier 1: good or better teaching for all

The key principle of Tier 1 support is that every teacher is a teacher of SEND. This approach goes beyond simply differentiating and adapting for individual students: it's about embedding inclusive practices and strategies across all aspects of school life. Good or better teaching is the minimum expectation in every classroom. This is a useful area to revisit each September, and something your SENDCo can lead on, referring to Section 6 of the SEND Code of Practice. It clearly highlights what is the class teacher's responsibility, what sits with the SENDCo, and where the two overlap.

Teachers are often surprised by how much falls into the 'teacher problem' category. Sometimes this is because their initial teacher training did not embed these expectations well; sometimes they aren't reminded enough; at other times, they have so many plates spinning that anything additional feels incomprehensible. I empathise with this, but in this instance, it is what it is. With the right SENDCo and senior leadership support, expectations should be at least good. However, I am sure that, as you read this, you can mentally place your teaching staff into different boxes depending on how well they meet these concepts. Try it now, using my favourite Carroll diagram.

	Willing	Unwilling
Able	Able & Willing	Able but Unwilling
Unable	Unable but Willing	Unable & Unwilling

Figure 3.1 The Able/Willing matrix is a great framework for categorising people across two dimensions: capability and motivation.

No doubt you also have a list of teachers who maintain a good teaching standard most of the time, and a list of those who currently do not. Getting most, if not all, of your teachers to this standard is key to effective classroom SEND provision. This might seem obvious, but many SENDCos are trying to embed good or better teaching for SEND students across the school *without* a whole-school strategy to raise all staff to this level.

It's not the SENDCo's role to single-handedly improve this situation; again, this is a whole-school issue. One SENDCo in my network likened trying to improve SEND provision in classes to 'putting a plaster on an amputation'. They felt completely isolated and demoralised. Although this scenario applies only to a minority of schools, the work required to improve teaching standards, especially during a teacher recruitment and retention crisis, shouldn't be underestimated.

The fundamentals of good or better teaching for SEND

Before we go further, let's look at what some key terms in education mean: adaptation, scaffolding and differentiation. These words are often used in similar ways, but they aren't the same. People sometimes use their own definitions, which can stray from the words' true meanings; one of my key bugbears in my line of work. In the next few paragraphs, I'll share how I understand these concepts.

Adaptive teaching

Adaptive teaching makes up the foundation of an inclusive classroom, where teachers adjust their strategies and resources to meet the varied needs of all students. Rather than using a one-size-fits-all approach, adaptive teaching recognises the need to tailor learning objectives to a diverse group of learners. At its heart, adaptive teaching is about flexibility. Teachers continually assess how students are engaging with the learning material and make the best possible adjustments based on this feedback.

The aim of adaptive teaching is to create a learning environment where all students have the opportunity to succeed. Teachers working within an adaptive teaching framework anticipate learning barriers and design lessons that are accessible to most students, with some providing more personalised support where necessary. This approach is underpinned by the 'assess, plan, do, review' cycle (Department for Education, 2014), which provides continuous feedback on students' progress. This allows teachers to identify any gaps in understanding early, enabling them to make real-time adjustments and concurrently plan for future lessons. Adaptive strategies might include flexible grouping, scaffolded learning tasks, adjusting the pace of instruction or providing pre-teaching for specific learners.

It's not just about reacting in the moment; teachers should consider possible adjustments during the planning phase, ensuring that adaptations are well thought out rather than improvised. This is an important point, as I feel that this concept, when introduced, went hand in hand with a lack of consideration at the planning stage, making it seem OK to adapt 'on the hop', which may involve the long-suffering LSA having to do it in the moment without receiving any planning beforehand. This isn't ideal. Having a solid plan for adaptations will help LSAs, as will providing training in strategies like chunking and dual coding, so they can support students effectively during lessons.

There's a common misconception that adaptations should always happen in real time within a lesson. While that's part of it, I always stress the importance of planning adaptations in advance as well. This way, teachers can prepare materials such as adapted activity sheets, sentence starters, key vocabulary and pre-teaching opportunities. The most effective adaptations involve both proactive planning and real-time adjustments during the lesson.

Where does differentiation come in?

While adaptive teaching and differentiation share similarities, they aren't quite the same thing. Differentiation typically involves making planned changes for specific groups of students, whereas adaptive teaching is more dynamic and responsive, with adjustments made based on how the class is engaging with the lesson.

In recent years, 'differentiation' has become a bit of a dirty word in some education circles. I've heard educators being criticised for using the term. However, it's crucial to understand the distinction between the two. Adaptation itself is nothing new; it's been a part of best practice and teaching standards for years. Differentiation is still appropriate and has never gone away.

Differentiation is key when an individual's learning can't be adapted in such a way that they can meet the objective. For a small group of students, this may be the case, particularly if the objective is not appropriate for them. For example, if they are more than two years below the expected level for their age or have SEMH (social, emotional and mental health) needs that prevent them from engaging with the curriculum in the same way. In these instances, differentiation could involve offering a different objective or a more personalised curriculum, such as one based on the Engagement Model (2020).

It's worth noting that differentiation is a form of adaptation, and both terms overlap in many ways. So yes, use both adaptive teaching and differentiation when necessary, and challenge anyone (often an Ofsted inspector) who suggests that differentiation is no longer a valid concept!

How does scaffolding fit in?

Scaffolding plays a vital role in both adaptation and differentiation, acting as a support structure to help students access and succeed with the learning material, regardless of their starting point. Think of it like a set of stabilisers on a bike: you wouldn't take them off too soon, but once the student is ready, you gradually remove them, allowing for more independence (and perhaps a few resilience-boosting scrapes along the journey!). Just like the stabiliser analogy, teachers should consider the best methods of scaffolding and how best to remove it gradually for a successful outcome.

In the context of adaptive teaching, scaffolding provides the support that helps students engage with the lesson at their current level, while also ensuring that the learning remains challenging. It's all about making the content accessible but not too easy – essentially, providing just enough support to help students complete the objective successfully.

For example, teachers might use:

- visual aids such as diagrams or pictures to support understanding
- think-alouds where teachers model how to solve problems or think through a task
- sentence starters or scaffolding questions to guide students' thinking and responses
- back-chaining where students are successful at the end of the task, which gradually reduces.

The key here is that scaffolding is dynamic; it's adjusted as students' understanding grows. As the lesson progresses, teachers gradually reduce the level of support based on how well the student is managing.

In terms of differentiation, when a student is on a personalised curriculum, their objectives may still need scaffolding. For some learners, for example, a task may need to be broken down into smaller, more manageable chunks (chunking). The goal is always to provide the right level of challenge, with the appropriate support, for each individual.

Ultimately, scaffolding is a key element of both adaptive teaching and differentiation. It helps ensure that every student, no matter where they are in their learning journey, can engage with the content and make progress. It's the safety net that allows teachers to meet students where they are, offering just enough help without doing the work for them. As students gain confidence and competence, ideally the scaffolding is gradually removed, allowing for greater independence.

Reflection questions

- How well does your school's universal provision support all students, including those with SEND, to receive good or better teaching?
- Are there any areas you feel could be developed further?

- Think about how you currently use adaptive teaching strategies in your school and classrooms – what's working well?
- Are there moments where you could plan adaptations a little more proactively, rather than responding in the moment?
- How do you tell the difference between adaptive teaching and differentiation in your planning?
- Do your staff feel confident in using both approaches to meet the needs of your students?
- Take a moment to think about how scaffolding is used in your lessons – do you feel you are giving students the right level of support?
- What barriers might be getting in the way of consistently delivering good or better teaching in your school or classroom, and what could you do to help address these, particularly for students with SEND?

4 Key classroom strategies

Getting started with universal approaches

Before we jump into specific strategies, it's helpful to remember that inclusive practice doesn't mean reinventing everything you already do. Most teachers are already using approaches that support a wide range of learners without necessarily labelling them as 'SEND strategies'. What matters is being intentional: noticing where small tweaks can remove barriers and building habits that make the classroom a more predictable, accessible place for everyone.

None of this is about perfection or elaborate plans. It's about having a clear starting point, knowing your pupils and using simple adjustments that make daily teaching smoother and more manageable. The following strategies offer practical ways to strengthen that foundation without adding unnecessary workload or complexity.

Differentiation and adaptation

Students come with varying needs, abilities and learning preferences. The concept of differentiation means that lessons, materials and assessments must be adapted to meet the diverse needs within the classroom.

For instance, a teacher might provide additional visual aids, scaffold writing tasks or adjust the level of questioning to ensure that all students can access the curriculum. Differentiation also involves recognising the individual learning needs of students, although this is now approached in a more evidence-based way rather than relying on outdated learning-styles theories. It's worth your SENDCo coordinating a bank of these resources for teachers and students to access, whether that is a class bank or a pack for individual students.

Universal Design for Learning (UDL)

The principles of UDL suggest that learning should be designed in a way that is accessible to all students. UDL encourages teachers to offer multiple means of engagement (e.g. through practical activities, discussion or independent study), representation (e.g. presenting information visually, verbally or through interactive media) and expression (e.g. allowing students to show their understanding in different ways, such as through writing, speaking or creative projects). There are many ways that learners can complete tasks, and this is not always needed. If learners have the option of using technology or a voice-note app, for example, they are taking ownership of their learning, which is highly motivational. This is good for all learners, and teaching strategies that are good for students with SEND benefit all students. See Part 2 for whole-school UDL strategies.

Formative assessment and feedback

Regular, formative assessments are essential in understanding how well students are progressing and where adjustments may need to be made. Teachers should engage in ongoing assessments, such as questioning, quizzes, peer assessment or self-reflection, to gauge how well students are grasping concepts. The feedback provided should be timely, constructive and aligned with clear learning outcomes. Teachers could use strategies such as mini whiteboards, low-stakes quizzes or a simple thumbs-up or thumbs-down throughout the lesson.

The classroom environment

The physical classroom environment should be inclusive and supportive, with accessible resources and seating arrangements that cater to diverse needs. This includes ensuring that students have access to materials such as reading aids (ideally some sort of reading pen), sensory tools or appropriate technology. A well-organised, positive and supportive classroom encourages both academic success and emotional wellbeing for all students. A key area here is the use of manipulatives in maths lessons: many students aren't keen to use them as they get older due to looking different from their peers. Manipulatives on the tables for all is a good way around this, as they can benefit all students.

Behaviour

A positive, consistent approach to behaviour is crucial in maintaining an inclusive classroom. Teachers should establish clear expectations for behaviour, using restorative approaches and positive reinforcement. For students with SEND, personalised strategies may be necessary, such as additional time to process instructions or access to quiet areas for reflection. It's worth reflecting on the inclusiveness of your behaviour policy and whether it needs a clause about reasonably adjusting unreachable standards for individual students (who would then need their own tailored version of the expectations). We will explore this further in Part 2.

Robust SEMH support

Again, this is a school-wide strategy which will be covered in more detail in Part 2. But the bottom line is: happy people learn better!

Tier 2: targeted support and intervention

While good or better teaching in Tier 1 forms the foundation of inclusion, there are times when individual students need additional support. Tier 2 interventions are designed to provide more detailed, targeted support for learners who require extra help beyond what is offered in mainstream teaching.

Tier 2 interventions are designed to be short-term (although, realistically, they often aren't) and aim to address specific barriers to learning (and again, realistically, these areas aren't always an easy fix). These interventions may focus on particular skills or areas where a student is struggling, such as literacy, numeracy or social communication. They may be for students on the SEND register but equally can be for anyone needing some extra support. When the interventions become more than a short term boost, that's when a student may need to be included on your SEND register.

Small-group interventions

Small-group work allows students to receive more focused support. Interventions might focus on areas like reading, writing or mathematics, and may or may not (depending on needs within the group) take place outside the general classroom environment. I have worked for leaders who insisted that all interventions must be in class because that is 'inclusion', despite one student having a hearing impairment and needing to be somewhere quiet.

Additional support for social or emotional needs

Some students will require additional support in managing emotions or improving social interactions. This might involve social-skills training or emotional-literacy programmes. Again, there is too much need for not enough resources, and tapping into local organisations such as MIND is very useful. Training someone in pastoral leadership, counselling or learning mentoring is highly beneficial. More on this in Part 2.

One-to-one support

For students with more complex needs, one-to-one support may be necessary. This could involve tailored interventions aimed at addressing very specific needs. For example, a student with speech and language difficulties might work with a speech and language therapist (a Tier 3 specialist intervention) to develop communication skills in a highly personalised way, then work one-to-one with an LSA on targets between sessions (Tier 2). A full-time 1:1 LSA for very complex needs would also come under Tier 3.

Tier 3 interventions: specialist support

Schools will need to work with external agencies such as speech therapists, educational psychologists or occupational therapists. These professionals can provide specialist advice, assessments and therapies that supplement the in-school support for Tier 3. Who pays for this is a moot point. Children needing Tier 3 support will be heading towards an Education, Health and Care Needs Assessment (EHCNA), or they will already have an EHCP in place. Extract as much money as you can from your LA and then see whether your budget will stretch to the specific areas of need in your setting. Then go back and extract some more if there is a shortfall.

Reflection questions

- What steps can you take to ensure your strategies support SEND students and help everyone in the class learn better?
- Are there tools or resources you could add or organise to make things easier for teachers?
- How could you adjust your teaching to give students more choices in how they take part, show what they know and share their learning?
- How might this boost motivation and help students, especially those with SEND, take more ownership of their learning?
- How do you use formative assessments now to check on student progress?
- Are there other simple assessment methods or feedback tools you could try to get quicker, more useful information about how students are learning?

5 When to seek specialist support

Most leaders will meet at least one pupil whose needs go beyond what mainstream can reasonably offer. Not because your provision isn't strong, or because staff lack skill but because some pupils need an educational model that mainstream simply wasn't designed to deliver.

Specialist provision is not the end of the road; it's a continuation of the same goal of giving a child access to learning, safety, dignity and long-term possibility. But identifying the moment when mainstream is no longer the right match can be difficult. This chapter helps you recognise those signs, build your case, work with families and understand what options are actually on the table.

What follows combines professional judgement, lived SENDCo experience, and the realities of current systems, including the rising thresholds, long waiting times and the need to build a watertight evidence base.

Needs that exceed what adaptation alone can achieve

Some pupils need specialist pedagogy rather than a heavier dose of mainstream support. You may notice:

- a pupil who requires continuous adult mediation for communication, safety or basic participation
- a developmental profile significantly younger than their chronological age, leading to sensory or social overwhelm
- a pattern of distress or disengagement that persists despite thoughtful adjustments
- levels of adult support that effectively create a 'micro-environment' within the classroom.

It's common for these pupils to 'manage' in primary, often because relationships are strong and the environment is predictable, but then hit a wall in secondary school. This doesn't mean the need was masked in primary; it reflects the fact that the secondary model is fundamentally different. Leaders benefit from acknowledging this openly.

Emotional needs that the mainstream ecosystem can't sustain

Some pupils' emotional worlds simply don't align with the noise, flux and social complexity of mainstream settings. You may notice:

- a pupil who spends more time recovering from the environment than engaging with learning
- ongoing dysregulation triggered by everyday events such as staff absence, timetable changes or loud, crowded spaces
- a pattern where the school day is shaped around preventing crisis rather than promoting learning.

In situations like these, specialist SEMH provision isn't a punitive move. It offers a quieter, more consistent ecosystem, integrated therapeutic routines, better adult-to-pupil ratios and a curriculum designed to respond to a pupil's emotional readiness.

Lack of progress, even with robust, high-quality intervention

One of the clearest signs a specialist setting may be appropriate is when a pupil's needs remain high *despite* sustained and well-delivered support across all tiers. Typical patterns include:

- consistent, monitored Tier 1 teaching
- targeted Tier 2 and Tier 3 interventions delivered with fidelity
- assess, plan, do, review (APDR) cycles that are purposeful and responsive, sometimes shortened because needs escalate quickly
- progress that is small, inconsistent or dependent on resources that aren't sustainable
- regression when any element of support is reduced.

The aim here isn't to demonstrate failure but to show that the current environment can't consistently meet need, even with high-quality practice in place.

Medical needs that require daily clinical insight

Some pupils have medical needs that mean specialist medical-educational settings are safer and more sustainable. This becomes clear when:

- a pupil's day involves medical interventions that exceed what mainstream can reasonably provide
- staffing requires medical training that can't be maintained with turnover or capacity
- health fluctuations make attendance, transition and curriculum access unpredictable
- the physical environment would need adaptations that aren't feasible.

Mainstream schools often support pupils with medical needs exceptionally well for many years. The moment of change usually comes when you find yourself trying to compensate for the absence of clinical expertise that specialist settings embed as standard.

How to build the case for specialist provision

Construct a coherent evidence narrative

Forget mountains of paperwork. Local authorities need a clear, accurate story of need. Your evidence narrative might include:

- **A communication profile:** How does the pupil communicate? How dependent are they on adult scaffolding?
- **A costed provision map:** This is vital. It paints a picture of sustainability.
- **Access to teaching:** Can the pupil access high-quality Tier 1 teaching? If not, is the barrier skill, environment or need?
- **An intervention record:** Which Tier 2 interventions have been implemented? Were they completed with fidelity? What changed?

- **APDR cycles:** Have these been regular, purposeful and responsive? Shortened cycles (e.g., fortnightly) can demonstrate rapidly emerging needs.
- **Behaviour and safety data:** A log of incidents, injuries or patterns that show risk isn't diminishing.
- **Developmental gap:** What is the gap between chronological and developmental age? Is it widening?
- **Personalisation:** Evidence of personalised timetables, environment adjustments, curriculum modification.
- **Tier 3 support:** What is in place? How sustainable is it?

Presenting provision in cost terms is not about budget justification; it shows the scale and sustainability of support required.

Assess impact on the pupil and on the school

A strong case reflects both the impact on the pupil: their academic progress, emotional wellbeing, physical safety, social connection; and the impact on others: the degree to which the pupil's needs reshape staffing, timetabling, or compromise the learning of classmates. This is the reality LAs need to see, presented calmly and professionally.

Resource evaluation

Leaders should ask:

- what additional resources are needed to meet the pupil's needs appropriately
- whether this is sustainable within mainstream funding
- whether the EHCP banding is accurate
- whether the EHCP reflects the pupil's current needs
- what it would take to maintain meaningful progress in mainstream.

Often, the conclusion isn't about willingness but about feasibility.

Specialist input (and how to use it strategically)

External professionals rarely state directly that a pupil requires specialist provision. However, their recommendations often imply:

- specific staffing ratios
- environmental adjustments such as low-arousal spaces or specialist equipment
- therapeutic input at a frequency mainstream can't deliver
- safety considerations that indicate a need for specialist staffing.

You can interpret these recommendations in context and use them to strengthen your case.

Working with health services

For pupils with medical needs:

- make early connections with relevant health professionals
- share well-organised information, including assessments and intervention records
- clarify roles and expectations, such as whether therapists provide direct work or staff training
- use multi-agency meetings to align plans
- keep clear written records of agreed actions
- support families in navigating health systems, which can be complex.

Strong collaboration can reinforce applications for specialist medical-linked provision.

The EHCP reality check

Every pupil being considered for specialist provision should have an EHCP. If they don't, start the process. If the EHCP is outdated, initiate an early review. Given current timelines in many areas, early action is a matter of safeguarding future options.

Understanding what specialist provision actually means

- Special schools are typically designated by primary need:
  - communication and interaction
  - cognition and learning
  - SEMH
  - sensory needs
  - physical disability.

Thresholds, resources and curriculum models differ between school types.

- Specialist resource provisions and enhanced resource bases offer targeted specialist input within a mainstream setting. They can be suitable for pupils who need more than mainstream can provide but don't require a full specialist environment.
- Alternative provision (AP) supports specific SEMH or behavioural needs. It's not a replacement for a special school and serves a different purpose.
- Medical specialist settings integrate clinical and educational expertise for pupils whose medical needs require coordinated care.
- Independent and non-maintained specialist schools are often required when local places are unavailable or when a pupil's profile is highly specific.

A leadership discussion tool

This isn't intended as a checklist but can be used as a series of prompts to support your professional judgement.

- What steps have we taken so far, and what results have we seen?
- What does the pupil need that this setting can't provide?
- Does the environment fail to meet the pupil's basic needs?
- What risks remain even when we use best practices?
- What do we need to keep the pupil safe, involved and learning?
- Can we keep this up without it impacting the wider community?
- What do parents and carers notice, hope for or worry about?
- How does the pupil talk about their experiences?
- What's likely to happen over the next year, and when the pupil moves to secondary school?
- Are we helping the pupil get ready for a meaningful future?

Reflection questions

- Which students are in class but not really engaging with the learning?
- Where are staff so stretched that the situation can't continue much longer?
- Are we taking a proactive approach to our EHCP processes, or are we mostly reacting to issues as they arise?
- Do families get clear information about specialist pathways early on?
- Are there students who might have better long-term outcomes if they were in a different setting?

6 Working with your local authority

Schools are being asked to support more pupils with complex needs, often without enough help. School leaders should know how to challenge their local authorities effectively. If you want more guidance, I offer a webinar that covers the law, case law, and provides letter templates. You can find more details on the companion website for this book.

There are times when, despite our best efforts, we can't meet the needs of a pupil with SEND in mainstream provision. We're being asked more frequently to take pupils whose needs are just not appropriate for mainstream settings. This is not only due to limited resources; mainstream schools are increasingly being asked to admit pupils with significant needs such as high levels of SEMH or severe learning difficulties. We want our pupils to thrive, not just survive. If, after careful reflection, your school concludes that you can't meet a pupil's needs, you must remain steadfast in your response to the LA. Even if you have been formally 'directed' to take a pupil, there are still legally binding measures you can take. There is also plenty you can do about other common LA concerns. I have yet to encounter an LA that works wholly within lawful parameters; they seem rarer than unicorn poo, but if yours does, please let me know!

Extracting more money from your LA

Section F of the Education, Health and Care Plan (EHCP) is where the specific provision required by the student is listed. It's critical that the support outlined in this section is clear, specific and quantified. Often, LAs underfund this section but the Children and Families Act 2014 (CAFA) legally binds the LA to deliver what is in Section F. If they fail to do so, they are acting unlawfully. Don't hesitate to challenge them if they try to cut corners.

When requesting funding, refer to CAFA Section 42, which mandates that LAs secure special educational provision for students with EHCPs. You can find model letters to use in your correspondence on the IPSEA and SEND Action websites.

If your LA refuses to provide additional funding, cite the SEND Code of Practice as well, which emphasises that provisions must be 'detailed and specific' (para. 9.69). Keep copies of all correspondence and, if necessary, consider taking legal action – sometimes the threat of this helps the LA to proceed in a more lawful manner.

It's often worth providing a costed provision map that outlines how you are meeting each part of Section F. If this section is too vague, then either use that to your advantage or send the EHCP back after an extra annual review for an improved Section F.

Obtaining specialist placements for students with severe SEND needs

For students with severe or complex needs, mainstream schools often aren't suitable and a specialist placement is required. The CAFA allows parents and schools to request these placements, but LAs can be reluctant due to the high costs involved and the crippling shortage of spaces.

Under CAFA Section 38, parents (or schools) can request an Education, Health and Care Needs Assessment (EHCNA) if they believe a student's needs can't be met in a mainstream setting. If the LA tries to deny a specialist placement, they must provide evidence that the placement isn't necessary; simply saying 'no' isn't enough. To strengthen your case, gather as much evidence as possible from educational psychologists, speech and language therapists and other medical professionals. When you submit this request, you can use model letters from the Council for Disabled Children or IPSEA. Links to these have been included on the companion website.

Refusing entry when consulted for a placement

Mainstream schools can refuse to accept a placement for a student with severe SEND needs if they genuinely can't meet the needs of the child. However, this decision must be justified carefully. If your school is in this position, consider carefully whether you could meet said needs with some adjustments and bear in mind that the student's paperwork may not accurately present their needs.

It's worth speaking to a range of sources such as the previous school and parents as well. Sometimes parents don't paint a very accurate picture either;

they may wish for their child to have a mainstream education despite educational professionals considering otherwise. This can be a challenge for schools to navigate, with a heavy legal weight placed on parental preference. On the other hand, a student may have had a challenging time at a previous setting and a fresh start somewhere more inclusive is all that's needed. LAs often send out a lot of consultations for one student, so it's also worth finding out whether your school is actually parental preference. I once spent hours on a detailed reply to say we could not meet need, only to find that parents had no intention of sending their son to us anyway. Now I always check before writing.

The CAFA sets the legal framework for this in Section 43, which outlines that a school can refuse a place if admitting the child would be 'incompatible with the provision of efficient education for others' and no reasonable steps can be taken to avoid this incompatibility. This shouldn't be used lightly but can be an option when specialist provision is truly needed.

If consulted about a placement, make sure you provide a robust rationale, citing the SEND Code of Practice (para. 1.39), and detail how the school can't meet the child's needs without detriment to other students. I advise taking screenshots of the relevant sections of the reports to show why the setting is incompatible. Again, you can seek free guidance from SOS!SEN or IPSEA for support on how to frame your response (again, you can find links on the companion website for this book). AI is also increasingly helpful within your school's appropriate-use parameters.

Securing an EHCNA

If a student is struggling without appropriate support despite Tier 1 and Tier 2 interventions, schools or parents can apply for an EHCNA, which is the first step in getting an EHCP. CAFA Section 36 sets the threshold for an EHCNA, which is 'whether the child or young person has or may have special educational needs, and it may be necessary for special educational provision to be made for the child or young person' (2014). This is a low threshold. LAs shouldn't reject assessments easily, but they often do. Don't take no for an answer.

If an EHCNA is refused, challenge the decision immediately. You can lodge an appeal through the SEND Tribunal. Your county may also have the option of mediation, which can be used before the tribunal. When going through this process with my son, I sat in the meeting and simply said, 'You know and I know that legally you have to assess, so please just do it or I will take this further.' Although they still tried to dig their heels in and say no, once I started the tribunal route they rolled over and agreed to assess.

You can use model letters from SOS!SEN or IPSEA to outline why the LA is acting unlawfully and ensure that you reference the legal threshold from CAFA. Don't allow LAs to push you around when it comes to funding, placements or assessments. They often rely on schools not knowing the law and can act unlawfully to save money. With the correct knowledge, you can ensure students get the support they are legally entitled to, even when the LA tries to deny it. Remember, persistence is key – as is knowing your legal rights. Much more detailed training, step-by-step guides and model letters for school leaders and SENDCos to use alongside case law 8 can be found on the companion website.

As a final thought on this matter, I do have some empathy for the LA's role and for the LA employees working in difficult circumstances with limited budgets. I also wonder how some of them sleep at night. As a profession, we need to stop taking no for an answer in this area and collectively make a stand to secure the funding our students deserve. I've heard of schools and trusts claiming back literally tens of thousands of pounds (and, in some cases, hundreds of thousands of pounds) for students and schools. If we were all persistent in this aim, we could secure adequate funding and send a message to the powers that be that SEND funding needs a desperate overhaul.

Reflection questions

- How well do you know your LA's processes and policies for funding, placements and assessments for students with SEND?
- How could your school improve communication with the LA, especially when supporting students with more complex needs?
- How confident do you feel about challenging your LA if they do not provide the resources your SEND students need?
- Can you think of any recent times when your school challenged, or could have challenged, the LA? What happened as a result?
- Has your school had situations where mainstream provision was not right for a student and a specialist placement was needed? How did you work with the LA in these cases?
- Do you feel confident about getting extra funding for Section F of EHCPs? What steps could you take to make sure the LA meets its legal duties here?

- How do you decide whether to refuse a placement if your school can't meet a child's needs? What extra information do you collect before making your final choice?
- Have you ever found that a student's paperwork did not match their actual needs? How did this affect your school's decision?
- How proactive is your school in applying for EHCNAs for students who aren't thriving with current support?
- If your LA rejects an EHCNA request, what steps would you take to challenge the decision? How could you improve your current practices in preparing for such situations?
- How could your school work with other schools or trusts to challenge the LA together and get better funding for SEND students?
- What could you do to make sure your school stays persistent when negotiating with the LA for the right support and resources?
- How can your school community take action to advocate for the funding and support SEND students need, both in your school and across the wider education system?

7 Supporting general SEND needs

The way you support students depends on your resources and how your class is set up. It also relies on your experience as a teacher, the number of students with additional needs in your class, and your school's structure and behaviour policy. No matter what you call it – 'high-quality teaching' (HQT), 'quality first teaching' (QFT) or another term – it all comes down to good teaching. When you make this a regular part of your practice, you can prevent most issues before they begin. In this book, I will call it 'best practice teaching' (BPT).

BPT is crucial for preventing classroom issues. It's first about ensuring that all staff are clear on their responsibilities, especially class teachers. Ultimately, the responsibility for student progress and assessment lies with the class teacher, not the SENDCo. Reminding staff of their roles ensures everyone is aligned. It also prevents SENDCos from doing more than coordinating. Of course, it may be that your SENDCo teaches and also takes on interventions depending on their skills and school preferences, but empowering your SENDCo to explain their role versus the teacher's role is a useful exercise for a September INSET.

Section 6 of the SEND Code of Practice says, 'Every teacher is a teacher of SEND' (2014). In other words, every classroom teacher is responsible for the progress and development of all their students, including those with SEND. It helps when your SENDCo reminds staff about the graduated approach APDR cycle: assess, plan, do and review. The NASEN version explains this clearly and shows what teachers need to do.

- **Assess**: in the 'assess' stage of the graduated approach – a cycle where support for students with special educational needs is regularly reviewed and improved – teachers develop a better understanding of each student's needs. A clear understanding of a child's needs is essential for planning effective teaching, deciding on appropriate support and making adjustments that help students make good progress and achieve better outcomes.
- **Plan:** during the 'plan' stage, teachers learn more about which teaching methods work best. This step is most effective when teachers and the SENDCo work together after carrying out a thorough assessment of a student's needs during the 'assess' phase.

- **Do:** in the 'do' stage, teachers refine their understanding of effective support. The SEND Code of Practice (2014) states that teachers are responsible for all students' learning on a daily basis and also sets out the SENDCo's role.
- **Review:** in the 'review' stage, teachers develop a clearer understanding of which approaches lead to better outcomes. Teachers should always monitor students' progress, both formally and informally, and this applies equally to students with SEND. Teachers do not need to wait for formal review meetings before making changes to teaching approaches or support where appropriate.

The class or subject teacher remains responsible for working with the child every day. Even if a student takes part in group or one-to-one sessions with another adult, the class or subject teacher still retains responsibility for the student. The SENDCo should support the class or subject teacher by assessing the child's strengths and weaknesses, helping with problem solving and advising on the effective implementation of support.

That's not to say we shouldn't support our teachers; we're all aware of the day-to-day plate spinning that classroom teaching involves. When the Code of Practice says 'every teacher is a teacher of SEND' (2014), this also includes SENDCos and school leaders, because we're all teachers.

A school-wide culture of inclusion and teamwork is essential. Everyone should have a clear understanding of their roles in supporting inclusion and SEND. Sometimes roles are discrete, such as the SENDCo leading an annual review, and sometimes they overlap, for example when a class teacher seeks advice from the SENDCo about a student.

From my experience, and from speaking with other SENDCos, I have seen many different types of class teachers. Some are highly effective, flexible and inclusive. Others believe that reasonable adjustments aren't actually 'reasonable' and assume that the SENDCo is solely responsible for the students with SEND in their class. These represent two extremes, and most teachers fall somewhere in between. Ideally, your staff sit closer to the inclusive end of the spectrum.

Your role

As a school leader, your role includes setting the inclusive climate and expectations of your staff and school, as well as empowering and supporting your SENDCo to have those difficult conversations with individual teachers whose inclusivity is lacking. This includes investigating and facilitating the resolution of parental complaints against staff in this area.

Occasionally a parent has brought a grievance to me about a staff member and I'm thinking, 'I can just imagine them doing or saying that'. After a discussion with the relevant parties, it's often the SENDCo's role to smooth the waters and re-establish a positive relationship between the parents and the teacher. With many staff grievances from parents, it's often a simple misunderstanding that's easy to rectify. Similarly, many students have needed to be held to account for untruths, bending of the truth, or leaving out key pieces of information they have relayed to their parents.

Ensuring BPT is consistent across the school

Back to BPT. I tell my SENDCos that if this is done well, it prevents problems before they start. Unfortunately, this is an area that schools struggle with consistently for a variety of reasons. For example, it could be the overall quality of teachers, inexperienced teachers or an issue caused by a high staff turnover. It's really important to keep reviewing regularly so that it's embedded effectively. Although I have very few positive things say about Ofsted, I did welcome a better emphasis on supporting students with SEND in class. Your teaching can't be good if you're not adjusting reasonably or adapting effectively for your learners' needs.

Here are some essential components for ensuring that your BPT is properly embedded:

- A robust staff induction (you could use pre-recorded webinars to outline school expectations).
- Ongoing training for LSAs and teachers, including time for researching and undertaking their own CPD according to personal needs.
- Listening to student voice and gathering their ideas about what would help them, how inclusive they feel their lessons are and whether they have a good relationship with key staff.
- Scaffolding essentials. This may include pre-teaching concepts, using a 'now and next' board or providing brain breaks.
- Accessible resources. This includes having laminated visual aids ready to use and ensuring LSAs can easily access tools such as mind maps or 'now and next' boards.
- Low-cost movement-break strategies, using outdoor areas where possible. Classrooms should also have designated safe spaces where students can retreat when they need a break.

- Brain breaks and sensory tools (i.e. fidget toys) that are readily accessible. Decide as a school how these are provided and ensure consistency across all classes.
- Accessible manipulatives for all students. These should be placed on tables within easy reach to encourage independence.
- A student concern form (see website), which helps staff document the best practice teaching strategies they have already tried before escalating a concern.

Differentiation

Although it has become somewhat of a controversial term, I still believe differentiation has a valuable place in education. As I see it, differentiation is what you do when a learner can't access the curriculum that most students are accessing in class, especially if they are more than two years below Age-Related Expectations (ARE) or have SEMH needs. In such cases, creating personalised timetables or tailored interventions is necessary. Of course, this requires adequate staffing and generally an EHCP application. The Engagement Model is useful here as it assesses students on their own objectives under the headings of:

- exploration
- realisation
- anticipation
- persistence
- initiation.

Gov.uk (2020) states that 'the model encourages schools to measure each student's progress independently, according to their individual profile of needs. It can also be used as a baseline tool to track and support ongoing progress'.

Nurture provisions

Some schools are getting creative with nurture provisions, which can span across year groups. However, it's important to ensure the age range is appropriate and that the right students are placed in the provision. You should also make sure that you're not trying to cater for too many areas of need at once. A provision linked to speech and language, for example, wouldn't be suitable for a student who is often dysregulated with SEMH.

It's also critical that nurture provisions remain connected to the wider school community. The students in these settings should still be part of their base class, and the individual student's class teachers should take an active role in their planning and assessment (as stated in the Code of Practice and APDR cycle), as well as visit the provision regularly. School leaders should also visit regularly to ensure the quality of provision and the support for the students and staff within it.

In my experience of visiting and supporting provisions, when they are isolated, staff feel undervalued and forgotten, as though they are simply managing students who are challenging in class. This is a particular issue if they have different breaktimes as well. That is not how it should be. Staff working in provisions should be trained well and guided by a qualified teacher, not left to it. Luckily, I have seen many more successful provisions than provisions that aren't working. In these, everyone has a shared vision and high aspirations for students. Staff aren't working alone and feel valued and supported in their roles.

I've worked with a variety of school leaders over the years and occasionally clashed with them about inclusive practices in school. As previously mentioned, in one school I worked in, the executive head ruled that all interventions must take place in the classroom in order to be 'inclusive'. While it's great to involve students in class activities, this approach doesn't always work for students with specific needs such as hearing impairments, speech and language needs or concentration difficulties. In these cases, quieter environments free from distractions are far more effective. This is just one example, but it highlights the need to have flexible policies when it comes to students with additional needs.

Reflection questions

- Do all teachers at your school use adaptive teaching strategies?
- Does everyone have a common understanding of terms like 'scaffolding', 'differentiation' and 'adaptation'?
- Do teachers adjust their teaching both before and during lessons? Are they thinking about individual students when planning?
- Is it clear from students' books how lessons have been adapted?
- What diagnostic assessment methods do you use, and are they working well?

- Do you have ways to share and celebrate successful strategies with other classes and families?
- Are there students who might benefit from a personalised timetable or an Engagement Model approach?
- Is there a need or possibility to set up a nurture provision for certain groups of students?
- Does everyone agree on what counts as a 'reasonable adjustment'?

Reasonable adjustments

Recently this term has been used more widely, and rightly so. In the UK, we're further behind some countries in terms of ensuring equal access. Japan, for example, is much further ahead than us in supporting people with disabilities. For instance, pedestrian crossings have two buttons: a high one and a low one. Although we're already doing a lot as a nation, and in our schools, there is more work to do.

Reasonable adjustments in education are defined as 'changes that organisations and people providing services must make if someone's physical or mental disability puts them at a disadvantage compared with others who aren't disabled' (Department for Education, 2023).

In a school context, the Department for Education (DfE) goes on to say, 'Schools have a legal obligation under the Equality Act to support students who are disabled with reasonable adjustments, making sure they can benefit from what the school offers in the same way as a student who is not disabled' (2023). Within the term 'disabled', they are also referring to students with SEND.

In practice, it can be a challenge for schools and leaders to identify the scope of the word 'reasonable'. What is reasonable – and at what point does reasonable become unreasonable? I have endeavoured to put together a guide to what reasonable adjustments could look like in your school. You can find my resources on reasonable adjustments via the companion website.

Making learning accessible for all

It's crucial to ensure that every child has what they need to succeed, and that includes providing materials in formats that work for them. Whether that means electronic textbooks, Braille or large print, it's about removing barriers. Using accessible technology is a game-changer. For example:

- pre-teaching new concepts gives students a head start
- mind mapping can help with knowledge retention and building vocabulary
- seeking specialist teacher advice for those students who need a bit more support
- creating a literacy-friendly classroom where everyone feels included
- using visual tools like 'now, next, then' boards and making time for brain breaks when attention starts to drift.

Extra time and space for assessments

When it comes to assessments, some students need a bit of extra time or space to perform their best. This is not about making things easier but about giving them what they need to succeed. It is all part of access arrangements, which apply to all assessments, not just the big exams. For example, an anxious student might need to complete assessments in a quieter, sensory-needs-friendly environment, or a student with literacy difficulties might need extra time and a scribe to support them.

Flexible seating

Seating arrangements can make a world of difference to a student's learning experience. Flexibility here is key to ensuring that all students are comfortable and have what they need.

For example:

- a visually impaired student may sit at the front with extra room for their equipment
- a student who needs a safe space might prefer to sit near the exit
- a hearing-impaired student could sit in a quieter area for group work
- a mixture of standing desks, seated desks or even beanbags could be used.

Assistive technology

We know that technology can really level the playing field for students with additional needs. Assistive technology, when used effectively, helps students engage in ways that work best for them. Students with working memory difficulties can use recording devices or voice-note apps, while another student might need a reading pen to access classroom texts. Someone else might do the bulk of their work on a laptop, focusing on building typing skills.

Adapting assignments

Assignments aren't one-size-fits-all, and it is important to adjust them where needed. This could mean scaffolding tasks or breaking them down into smaller, more manageable steps, such as providing sentence starters, scaffolded sheets or word mats to give students a starting point, or allowing students to choose how they complete a task, with a couple of options, giving them some control over their learning. if a task doesn't fit, a personalised curriculum or alternative objective may be appropriate.

Note-taking and communication support

Some students need a bit more support with note-taking and communication. Offering alternatives can make a huge difference to their learning experience. For example, students can take notes as a group and share them so no one misses out, or one person could be the magpie, tasked with pinching information from other groups using communication boards, visual cards or lanyards to support those with hearing impairments or communication needs. Other students might benefit from extra adult support to help them organise ideas, take notes or ease communication.

Physical accessibility

It's essential to make sure the physical environment works for everyone. This might include ensuring pathways are clear and using ramps for mobility. For example:

- check that students can move around the building without issues
- keep pathways clutter-free for students with mobility challenges
- add Braille or symbols to displays if needed.

Individual plans and needs

Not every student fits neatly into the whole-school behaviour policy. Some need a more tailored approach, and that's okay. Individual Education Plans (IEPs) are essential for ensuring their needs are met. Universal provision should also be considered. For example:

- a student might use ear defenders or have access to a mindful area
- they may have their own SEMH support plan instead of following the school's main one
- some students might enter and exit the building at different times or through different routes to avoid overstimulation.

Small changes, big impact

These adjustments appear small on their own, but they can make a world of difference for students with additional needs. Not only do they help with learning, but they boost confidence and help students feel like valued members of the school community. It's also vital to include a diverse range of students in student voice initiatives to explore inclusivity even further from their perspective. So often we steam ahead and put in place what we think would benefit the student without even asking them!

Reflection questions

- How well are adaptive teaching strategies integrated into everyday classroom practice at your school?
- Do all staff share a clear understanding of key terms such as scaffolding, differentiation and adaptation?
- Are teachers actively adapting their teaching both during planning and as lessons progress, based on the needs of specific learners?
- Can you observe clear adaptations or personalised strategies in student books, reflecting inclusive teaching practices?
- What diagnostic assessment processes are in place to identify student needs, and are they effectively supporting all learners?
- How are successful inclusive strategies shared across classes and celebrated with both staff and families?
- Are there any students who could benefit from a personalised timetable or the use of the Engagement Model to track progress more effectively?
- Is there a need or capacity within your school to establish a nurture provision for targeted groups of learners?

- Do all staff have a clear understanding of what constitutes a 'reasonable adjustment' and how to apply this in practice?
- Are all members of staff aware of their legal obligations under the Equality Act to support students with disabilities and SEND through reasonable adjustments?

8 An overview of common areas of need in school

Supporting neurodivergent pupils is now an essential component of effective school leadership. While the presentation of needs such as ADHD, autism, dyslexia, Developmental Language Disorder, dyspraxia and sensory processing differences can vary wildly, they share one important feature: each can shape a pupil's experience of learning, behaviour and belonging in school. As a school leader, your challenge is less about becoming an expert in every condition (impossible and exhausting) and more about understanding the patterns that commonly affect classroom life, and ensuring that your staff feel equipped, confident and supported to respond.

This chapter takes a strategic approach: first outlining the universal leadership actions that benefit most neurodivergent pupils, then highlighting specific considerations for individual conditions. This structure will help you to implement broad, inclusive systems while being alert to needs that require specialised responses.

Universal leadership actions

These leadership actions benefit virtually all neurodivergent pupils. Rather than implementing them separately for each condition (which would be unmanageable), as a starting point, embed them as standard practice across your school and then overlay specific adjustments for specific students.

Environment and sensory adjustments

There are a variety of environmental amendments that can make a massive difference to a significant proportion of your students. What helps neurodivergent students generally helps everyone (or at the very least, does not hinder them). Consider all aspects of your school, such as those flickering fluorescent lights that may trigger migraines for students with sensory processing difficulties.

The physical environment

Start by exploring your classrooms and school through a sensory lens. Walk around with your SENDCo and notice the environment. Is there constant background noise? Could you reduce it through some basic adjustments – carpets, curtains, closing doors and windows?

Good lighting matters, not just for students with visual impairments. Where possible, ensure lighting lighting doesn't create glare on whiteboards or screens, and be aware that, for some students, certain types of lighting can be physically painful.

Something simple that makes a surprising amount of difference is maintaining consistent classroom layouts. Try to avoid moving the furniture around where possible: for students with visual impairments, it's a safety issue. For students with neurodiversity or SEMH, it's an anxiety trigger. For everyone, it's just easier to navigate a space when things stay where you expect them to be. If spaces are changed, give key students warning about what changes will look like and who they will be sitting with. Mark edges and obstacles with high-contrast colours – a roll of yellow tape on stair edges can be helpful. Provide accessible signage with clear fonts.

Quiet spaces

Create designated low-stimulation areas where students can retreat when overwhelmed. The key word here is 'designated' - there needs to be a proper space with a proper system. Ensure these spaces are available without stigma. If students feel ashamed for needing a break, they won't want to take the opportunity. Train all staff in when and how students access these spaces, because if only some staff understand or buy into the system, it won't work. It needs to be a whole school initiative.

Don't forget to consider sensory issues in your dining hall. Lunchtime can feel like absolute chaos for some students - the noise, the smells, the unpredictability. Think about seating options, noise levels, whether there's anywhere calmer students can eat if the main hall is too much. I'm not suggesting you run a separate dining room (though some schools do), but acknowledge that lunchtime is overwhelming for some students and see what small adjustments you can make.

Seating and positioning

Flexible seating arrangements should ideally be available for all. Position students to minimise distractions, away from doors, windows and high-traffic areas. Allow students to sit where they can see and hear effectively. Where possible, provide options like single desks, workstations facing walls, or proximity to the teacher, depending on individual needs. Consider sensory preferences too - that squeaky chair might be causing an extra underlying sensory issue, and they might not even realise that's why they can't concentrate.

Visual supports everywhere

Implement visual timetables in every classroom. Not just in EYFS, not just for 'certain students' – everywhere. Use dual coding (words plus images) consistently; it helps everyone learn more effectively. Display key vocabulary, sentence starters and word banks. Make language visible. If your school uses knowledge organisers, ensure they are appropriately adapted for key students.

How you'll know if it's working

Take regular learning walks where you look at the environment, not just the lesson. Ask staff for feedback – they'll tell you if something isn't working. Most importantly, ask students. They're the experts on what helps them. Create simple environmental checklists to support this. Also, pay attention to incident data – if behaviour incidents spike in particular spaces or at particular times, also consider underlying environmental factors.

Structure, routine and predictability

Surprises rarely support children during the school day. That doesn't mean everything needs to be rigid or over-controlled, things change, and some flexibility is always needed.

But where you can, build in predictability. All these micro moments of predictability support the prevention of dysregulation.

Establish clear routines

Create predictable daily structures across the school which evolve through year groups and are predictable within each context. The key is consistency, so if you say something will happen at a particular time, make it happen at that time. Ensure smooth transitions between lessons and activities, because the unstructured nature of transition times is when students get overwhelmed and dysregulated.

Develop clear protocols for changes to routine, because things do have to change sometimes. Fire drills happen. Assemblies get moved. Supply teachers arrive. The difference is in how you communicate these changes. Give as much warning as possible. Use visual timetables to show what's different. Don't just announce 'By the way, we're doing something completely different in five minutes' and expect everyone to cope seamlessly.

Communicate expectations clearly

Ensure all staff communicate expectations explicitly. Say what you mean and mean what you say, which sounds obvious, but we're all guilty of vague instructions: 'Get ready for assembly' (ready how?), 'Line up nicely' (what does *nicely* mean?), 'Do your best work' (what does that look like?). Be specific. Break information into manageable chunks, too.

Check for understanding, but do it explicitly. 'Do you understand?' is not ideal as everyone inevitably says yes. Ask students to explain it back to you. Get them to show you what they're going to do first. Use consistent language across the school, especially when it comes to actioning your behaviour policy.

Prepare for transitions

Build adequate time into timetables for movement between spaces within the school day, upon entering school in the morning and home time. Those children who are experiencing school avoidance need particular support in entering the school building. Plan properly for transitions from one key stage to another – EYFS to Year 1 is a massive leap and needs to be planned particularly carefully. Work with previous settings to prepare for new students; don't wait until they arrive to start thinking about their needs. Similarly, ensure your Year 6–7 (and sometimes Year 2–3) transitions are also taking into account those with additional needs. Consider transition books and extra opportunities to build relationships with new staff. Work closely with parents and carers and previous staff on this as well.

How you'll know if it's working

Observe transition times – this is where you see what's really happening. Track incidents – if behaviour problems spike during transitions or after routine changes, you know where to focus. Ask staff for feedback on consistency – are you all actually doing what you said you'd do? Pay attention to student stressors. If students are constantly anxious about what's happening next, they need more predictability.

Staff training and whole-school understanding

As you are already aware, supporting students with SEND isn't just your SENDCo's job. It's everyone's job. From the headteacher to the site manager to the midday assistants (who often have some of the most valuable insights about your students because they see them in unstructured social situations).

Train everyone

Make inclusion and SEND training mandatory for all staff. Include support staff, midday supervisors, the admin team: literally everyone who interacts with students. The school office manager needs to understand student inclusion needs too, because students interact with them, and a compassionate, understanding response in the office can make a real difference to an anxious child.

Provide ongoing CPD, not just one-off sessions. One INSET day won't make anyone an expert. This needs to be embedded, revisited and built up over time. Cover understanding, empathy and practical strategies. Make sure training includes how different conditions present differently. Autism in girls, for instance, has previously been regularly missed because we're looking for boys' presentation patterns.

Build confidence

Create opportunities for staff to share what's actually working in their classrooms. Your Year 3 teacher might be doing something your Year 5 teacher really needs. That only happens if you've built a culture where asking for help is normal, not something to hide. If staff feel they can't say they're struggling, they'll just get on with it quietly and the quality dips across the board.

Use real examples from your own setting. What has actually worked, with your pupils, in your classrooms. That will always land better than something picked up from a course. Staff need to see it in action, not just hear about it in theory.

Also, 'just add this in' with no time attached isn't a strategy. If you want staff to adapt their teaching well, you have to give them the time to think, plan and do it properly. Then recognise it when it's done well.

Develop specialist knowledge

Train key staff more deeply in specific conditions. Build expertise within your team. Ensure your SENDCo has relevant qualifications and, crucially, an appropriate amount of time to actually do the job. The SENDCo should be coordinating how staff connect with speech and language therapists, EPs, specialist teachers and other professionals. This isn't something the SENDCo should be holding alone or working through in isolation.

Put systems in place across the school so that specialist advice is shared, understood and used by the people who actually need it day to day. Advice shouldn't sit with one person or in one file. If it's not reaching staff, it's not making a difference.

How you'll know if it's working

Survey staff confidence levels (anonymous is better – you want honest answers; not what people think you want to hear). Look at the quality of IEPs and support plans – are they actually useful with achievable but aspirational, measurable and time bound targets? Triangulate with staff discussion, learning walks and SENDCo input. If the same issues keep arising, training hasn't been effective.

Communication systems

Communication sits at the heart of everything we do. Get this right and a lot of the day-to-day challenges reduce straight away.

Staff need to be supported to use clear, concise language. That means speaking at a steady pace, keeping sentences short and structured, and getting to the point. Then giving pupils time to process before expecting a response.

Silence isn't something to rush in and fill. Often it's thinking time. We need to get more comfortable with that.

Multi-modal communication

Supplement verbal communication with visual aids, symbols, written instructions. Provide information in multiple formats because different students need different inputs. Some need to hear it, some need to see it, some need to read it, ideally all three. Use gestures and facial expressions appropriately.

Implement communication aids where needed – Picture Exchange Communication System (PECS), speech-to-text, Augmentative and Alternative Communication (AAC) systems. Technology is your friend. These are all excellent reasonable adjustments.

Check understanding properly

Support staff to check understanding, not just compliance. 'Thumbs up if you understand' doesn't tell you as much as you may think! Pupils may just go with the majority! Build in ways to actually see what they've understood.

Where it helps, use choices rather than open-ended questions. 'Pen or pencil?' is often more effective than 'What do you want to use?' because it reduces the demand and supports decision-making.

Make it safe for pupils to say they don't understand. If it feels risky to ask, they'll stay quiet and carry on without it.

Support social communication

Explicitly teach social communication skills like turn-taking, active listening, understanding non-verbal cues. Don't assume students will pick them up by osmosis. Some will, many won't. Use social stories to explain expected behaviours in different situations. These are brilliant and underused.

Provide structured social opportunities. Some students need scaffolding for social interaction: implement buddy systems and peer support, but structure them properly. When you have used all the ideas you have with little progress, it's time to get a specialist involved.

How you'll know if it's working

Ask students for feedback on their understanding. Observe communication in classrooms – are instructions actually clear or are students constantly confused? Analyse incidents – communication breakdowns often lead to SEMH instances. Get parent feedback – if parents are confused about what's happening, students probably are too.

Positive behaviour and emotional regulation

Trying to 'manage' behaviour all day is exhausting, and it's not where the focus should sit.

For many pupils, particularly those who are neurodivergent, behaviour is communication. If we stay at the level of control and compliance, we miss what's actually going on and nothing really shifts.

Short-term compliance might look like it's worked, but it rarely builds understanding, independence or trust. If anything, it can make things harder over time.

The focus needs to move towards understanding, support and teaching the skills behind the behaviour, not just reacting to what we see in the moment.

Create an inclusive behaviour policy

Review your behaviour policy to ensure it supports all learners. If your policy only works for students who respond well to traditional rewards and consequences, it's not fit for purpose. This doesn't mean having no expectations or consequences – it means understanding that some students need different approaches.

Allow for individualised adaptations where needed. Yes, this means some students will have adjusted expectations. Fair doesn't mean identical; fair means everyone gets what they need to succeed. Focus on the behaviour, not the child. 'That didn't work' rather than 'You are naughty.' The child is not the problem; the behaviour is communication. Use relational, restorative approaches. Consequences alone rarely teach what we think they do.

Train staff in co-regulation techniques. You can't calm a dysregulated child if you're dysregulated yourself. Staff need to be able to manage their own emotions and remain calm even when students aren't. This is a skill that needs teaching and practising. Training can also support in our home lives as well!

Support emotional regulation

Implement whole-school regulation strategies – the *Zones of Regulation* programme (accompanied by my Feelings Furballs), whatever works for your context. Teach emotional literacy across the school. If students can't identify and discuss their emotions, they can't regulate them effectively.

Provide toolkits for individual students – sensory circuits, reflection cards, calming strategies. What works for one student won't work for another, so personalisation matters. Train staff to recognise escalating anxiety and intervene early.

Create personalised behaviour support plans where needed. Generic approaches won't work for complex needs. Some students need very specific, individual strategies. Again, seek support of a specialist where needed.

Use positive reinforcement effectively

Embed a culture of specific, frequent praise. 'Well done' is meaningless. 'I noticed you waited patiently for your turn even though that was really hard' is great. Focus on effort and specific achievements, not just outcomes. Trying hard matters, even when the result isn't perfect.

Build strong student-adult relationships as the foundation of everything. If a student doesn't feel liked and valued, your behaviour strategies won't work. Work toward intrinsic motivation, not just external rewards. We want students to want to behave well because it feels good, not just because they get a sticker (I have a strong dislike of sticker charts).

Safe spaces and de-escalation

Provide quiet reflection spaces. Train all staff in de-escalation techniques. Use private signals to redirect dysregulation. Public call-outs just add humiliation to the problem, making things worse. Remain calm and solution-focused. Your regulation is the foundation for theirs. Allow time for students to regain composure. Once a student is dysregulated, they need time to regulate themselves.

How you'll know if it's working

Look at behaviour incident data – are things improving or the same issues recurring? Track exclusions and suspensions – if it's always the same students, your system isn't working for them. Survey staff confidence in SEMH support – struggling staff need support, not judgment. Ask students about their wellbeing – are children actually feeling safe and supported?

Teaching and learning adaptations

What supports students with SEND, supports everyone everyone – we've just got to be more intentional about it.

Break down learning

Ensure tasks are chunked into manageable steps. Provide step-by-step guides and checklists. Use scaffolding consistently. Pre-teach key vocabulary because you can't access learning if you don't understand the words being used. Allow processing time.

Use multi-sensory approaches

Encourage hands-on, interactive learning. Sitting still and listening only works for some students, and only for limited periods. Incorporate movement into lessons. Use visual resources extensively. Provide tactile learning opportunities where appropriate. Let students touch, build, manipulate.

Build in flexibility

Allow alternative ways to demonstrate understanding. Written work is not the only way to show learning. Drawings, models, technology, oral presentations are all valid. Provide choice in tasks where appropriate. Match tasks to students' strengths. Success builds confidence, and confidence builds more success.

Provide organisational support

Provide organisational tools – planners, timers, checklists, colour-coded folders. Executive function is genuinely hard for many students, so train staff in supporting executive function difficulties.

How you'll know if it's working

Do learning walks where you look for these strategies being used. Check work scrutiny – what's actually being produced? Look at progress data – are students making progress? Ask students what helps – and offer a variety of tools to try.

Technology and resources

Technology doesn't solve everything, but it's a hugely useful tool when used properly. Provide access to laptops, tablets or specialist software. Train students in using technology as early as possible, especially typing skills – Year 2 or 3, not Year 6 so that students are able to use technology with ease, which supports better outcomes, especially in English. Ensure digital content is accessible. Commission specialist technology assessments where needed. Sometimes you need expert advice on what technology would actually help.

Make materials accessible

Provide materials in multiple formats – paper, digital, audio, whatever works. Ensure clear, uncluttered layouts. Busy pages are exhausting to process. Use high-contrast colours. Provide enlarged or adapted resources as needed.

Allocate resources strategically

Budget for specialist equipment. If a student needs something to access learning, that's not a 'nice to have,' it's a necessity. Train staff in using specialist resources, because the laptop is ineffective if no one knows how to set it up or troubleshoot when it doesn't work. With so many students with literacy difficulties, technology such as a laptop and scanning pen is imperative to securing their success in literacy.

How you'll know if it's working

Check equipment usage data – is it sitting in cupboards or actually being used? Look at student outcomes with and without technology – does it make a difference? Ask staff for feedback on resource availability – are they getting what they need? Review technology assessment recommendations – are you actually following expert advice?

Partnerships and collaboration

Collaboration is key. The schools that are doing this well are the ones that have built strong teams, use their networks effectively, and work with parents as partners rather than adversaries.

Working with external specialists

Build relationships with educational psychologists, speech and language therapists, occupational therapists, specialist teachers. Don't wait until crisis point to make contact. Coordinate regular reviews. Consider commissioning your own specialists where budget allows; having a speech and language therapist come in once every half term might be more reliable than waiting for LA provision, which can be... variable.

Partnering with parents

Maintain regular communication with families, with a clear emphasis on positives as well as concerns. If contact only happens when there is a problem, the relationship is already under strain. Involve parents in shaping support plans and take time to listen to their perspectives.

Share strategies that are effective both at home and in school. Provide workshops and accessible resources so families feel informed and empowered, not just updated. It also matters that parents feel you genuinely value their child.

Support families through clear signposting to external services. Many are unaware of what is available or how to access it, and schools play a key role in bridging that gap.

Multi-agency working

Coordinate with health services, social care, external agencies because everyone needs to know what everyone else is doing. Streamline meetings where possible by combining IEPs, Team Around the Family (TAF) meetings or specialist visits. Avoid families repeating themselves to five different professionals.

Peer support

Implement buddy systems with clear purpose and structure. Support all pupils to understand difference in age-appropriate ways; this builds empathy and inclusion.

Create planned opportunities for structured peer interaction, recognising that some pupils need scaffolding to develop and maintain friendships. Monitor peer relationships carefully. Difficulties can be subtle, so it's important to stay aware and respond early.

How you'll know if it's working

Seek feedback from parents to gain honest, meaningful insight. Review multi-agency meeting minutes to ensure genuine collaboration is taking place.

Check whether specialist advice is being implemented in practice, rather than remaining in reports or files. Monitor the quality of relationships with families and professionals for effectiveness.

Condition-specific considerations

Now that you've got those key pillars sorted (or at least on your to-do list), here's what's actually different for each condition. This is the bit where you fine-tune, not rebuild from scratch. Remember, these build on the universal foundations – they're additions, not replacements.

ADHD

According to NHS data, around five per cent of children and young people in England display traits of ADHD (House of Commons Library, 2025). The road to diagnosis is long and many students will display ADHD traits alongside other additional needs such as autism. Your role is to ensure your staff have both understanding and empathy, creating a supportive environment.

Understanding the presentation

Students with ADHD typically experience challenges with organisation and self-regulation. While diagnostic descriptions group ADHD into three broad presentations, real students rarely fit neatly into fixed categories.

- *Inattentive*, which covers difficulty following instructions and focusing, as well as organising tasks. These students would not typically be described as hyperactive or impulsive.
- *Hyperactive/Impulsive presentation*, which presents as excessive activity, impulsive actions and difficulty sitting still or waiting for turns.

- *Combined presentation*, which is a combination of inattention and hyperactive/impulsive behaviours. This often leads to the most severe challenges.

What's different for ADHD beyond the universal

- **Movement and activity needs:**
  - Build movement breaks into lessons systematically. These students' brains work better when their bodies can move. Create opportunities for controlled physical activity – sending them on errands, using sensory trails around school, allowing them to stand while working.
  - Don't assume a child should keep going just because they can. Physical and mental fatigue are real, and students with ADHD often work much harder than their peers to achieve the same results because they're constantly fighting their own brain's desire to do something else.
- **Managing impulsivity:**
  - Train staff to understand that impulsivity is neurological, not wilful. They're not choosing to blurt out answers or touch things they shouldn't – their brain's just faster than their brakes.
  - Use private signals for redirection. Public call-outs just add shame to the problem. Accept that students may not be able to explain why they did something. 'I don't know' is often genuinely honest, not defiant. Focus on solutions, not blame. What happened has happened; what are we doing next?
- **Enhanced organisational support:**
  - Provide extra organisational tools – timers, checklists, planners. Executive function is genuinely hard. Many teachers mistake poor executive function for laziness, and that helps nobody. Use sticky notes and visual reminders everywhere to reduce the memory load.
- **Homework and assessment considerations:**
  - Review your homework policy specifically for ADHD. Sometimes reduced volume or alternative formats make more sense. Let students demonstrate understanding however works best for them.
- **Self-esteem is critical:**
  - Monitor for negative feedback loops. Constant correction destroys confidence, and students with ADHD often face more correction in a day than neurotypical students face in a week. Ensure staff reinforce that the behaviour is the issue, not the child.

- Build strong relationships. If students don't feel liked, nothing else works. Celebrate small successes because they need to know they can do things right, not just hear about everything they're doing wrong.

What to watch for

Self-esteem issues, friendship difficulties (impulsivity can make social situations tricky), organisational challenges that are getting worse not better, impulsive incidents, and honestly, teacher frustration levels (which will improve with training and empathy).

Autism

Supporting students with autism in schools requires an empathetic approach that recognises the unique challenges they face. I would recommend that everyone on your staff gets to try a sensory experience that helps people understand what it's like to live with autism. You can book a mobile bus that visits your school. After trying this, my empathy levels were certainly improved. Of course, every student with autism is different, so strategies should be considered to support the individual's needs, focusing on communication, sensory sensitivities and social interaction. Here are some key strategies to consider.

Understanding the presentation

Students with autism often have challenges with social communication and interaction, though what this looks like varies enormously. They need routine and predictability, because we're talking genuine distress when things change unexpectedly, not just preference. Many have sensory sensitivities, which can be hyper-sensitive (overwhelmed by sounds, lights, textures) or hypo-sensitive (seeking out sensory input), sometimes both for different things.

Crucially, autism is often masked, especially in girls. This is exhausting for students and means their needs are frequently missed because they appear to be coping when actually they're falling apart internally.

What's different for autism beyond the universal

- **Literal language is critical:**
  - Train all staff to be literal and explicit. This goes beyond clear communication. When you say 'in a minute,' that needs to actually mean

in a minute, not 'sometime in the vague future.' Reduce idioms (but also explicitly teach), sarcasm and implied meaning school-wide.

 - Explain jokes and figurative language explicitly. What seems obvious to neurotypical people can be genuinely confusing to students with autism. They're not being difficult; they genuinely don't understand the implied meaning.

- **Predictability needs enhancing:**
  - Communicate changes to routine well in advance – more notice than you'd give other students. Provide detailed information about what will happen. Use tools such as transition books where needed.
- **Sensory environment is heightened importance:**
  - Audit for specific sensory triggers. Allow sensory breaks proactively, not just reactively. Provide spaces where students can go when things get too much.
- **Social interaction needs explicit teaching:**
  - Implement structured social skills teaching, not just peer support. Many things that neurotypical students pick up automatically need to be explicitly taught to students with autism.
  - Use Lego therapy or similar structured interactions. Play with rules is easier than freeform play.
  - Teach understanding of non-verbal cues explicitly.
  - Allow choice about whether students present their needs to peers. Some want to explain, some absolutely don't.
- **Communication alternatives:**
  - Some students need Picture Exchange Communication Systems (PECS) or other AAC systems.
  - Allow extra processing time. Many autistic pupils need longer to process language and formulate a response, particularly in busy or language-heavy environments.
  - Work closely with speech and language therapists because autism isn't just about social communication; it's about language processing too. Implement specialist recommendations consistently.

What to watch for

Masking (especially in girls), anxiety levels, periods of overwhelm, social isolation and home-school behaviour differences.

Autism in girls

We are still catching up when it comes to autism in girls, this is because the majority of research into autism has focused on boys. In turn, this has shaped a significant amount of previous understanding about how the condition presents. As a result of this, many girls and women have not had their needs recognised or have been misdiagnosed. This has led to a delay in receiving support and intervention. If your team can be aware of how autistic traits present in both girls and boys, this can support everyone.

- Girls with autism are often far better at masking than boys, which means their needs go unrecognised for years. Take it seriously when girls appear fine at school but struggle at home. It's not 'poor parenting', it's more like a child holding it together all day and releasing when they feel safe.
- Look for girls who rely on others for social guidance, or often follow a peer's lead in group situations.
- Look for socially acceptable obsessive interests that don't raise flags the way boys' interests do. Being an avid reader is socially acceptable, but if a girl must read every single book by an author in a particular order, that's potentially more than just a love of reading.
- Watch for friendship struggles, passivity (which is seen as 'good' behaviour but might actually be overwhelm), and emotional outbursts, particularly after school or at home.
- Provide end-of-day debriefing opportunities. Let students release pressure in a controlled way before going home.
- Train midday supervisors to watch for vulnerabilities. Girls with autism can be easily led by peers, which creates real safeguarding risks. Initiate referrals promptly if you have concerns.

Social, Emotional and Mental Health

Supporting students with SEMH needs requires a school-wide approach embedded in daily practice. It takes significant time and perseverance to get these strategies working effectively. Relationships with key adults are vital, so ensure the right adults are allocated as far as is practicable. Progress can be so incremental that you don't notice until you look back three months later, but all progress *is* progress. Building SEMH foundations is the highest priority because without these, there's nothing to build learning on.

Understanding the presentation

Students with SEMH often have underlying anxiety, trauma or external factors affecting their wellbeing. There's always a reason, even if we don't know what it is. They may present as challenging behaviour or withdrawal – fight, flight or freeze responses. These students often need both in-house and external support, though external support is increasingly difficult to access with current waiting times.

What's different for SEMH

- **Early identification systems are crucial:**
  - Implement the Graduated Approach (assess, plan, do, review) rigorously.
  - Use behaviour support documents to identify triggers and patterns because behaviour is communication – work out what students are trying to tell you.
  - Work on transitions before students arrive, especially from preschool. Don't wait until September to start thinking about complex SEMH needs.
  - Support preschools with EHCP applications. They often need help navigating the process. Ensure appropriate students are on your SEND register.
- **The Graduated Response needs clear protocols:**
  - Create clear structures for in-house support because you can't rely on external services arriving quickly. Build your own capacity.
  - Develop protocols for when to refer versus when to manage in-house. You need clear thresholds.
  - Plan for part-time timetables and school avoiders. Sometimes reduced timetable is better than no timetable, and trying to force full attendance can make things worse.
  - Address emotional-based school avoidance (ESBA) proactively. It escalates fast so early intervention matters.
- **Emotional regulation is intensified:**
  - Provide personalised toolkits – sensory circuits, reflection timecards, calming strategies. What works for one student won't work for another, so individualisation matters.

    - Ensure staff can recognise signs of escalating anxiety. Learn the early warning signs – what does 'starting to struggle' look like for each child?
    - Train specifically in co-regulation techniques for SEMH. You're the calm in their storm.
    - Provide access to learning mentors. Sometimes students just need one safe adult they can talk to.
- **Build in-house capacity:**
    - Develop learning mentor provision.
    - Create in-house counselling or pastoral support because external waiting lists are brutal. Child and Adolescent Mental Health Services (CAMHS) referrals can take months or even years. Build staff expertise rather than relying solely on external services. You need to be able to act while waiting for specialists.
    - Provide clinical supervision models for staff supporting SEMH students. This work is emotionally demanding; staff need support too, or they'll burn out.
- **Student voice matters:**
    - Use Student Voice Confidence Questionnaires or similar tools. Ask students what they need. Empower students to communicate their needs in whatever way works – some can't tell you in words but can show you in other ways.
    - Involve students in creating their own support plans. Their buy-in matters enormously.
    - Consider the impact of individual SEMH needs on other students. One student's behaviour can affect the whole class; acknowledge this and support other students too.
- **External partnerships remain critical:**
    - Build relationships with educational psychologists, CAMHS and counsellors. These relationships take time; where possible, start those relationships as early as you can.
    - Access Specialist Teaching and Learning Services (STLS) where available.
    - Support families with school nurse referrals. Sometimes families need help they don't even realise is available or sometimes parental literacy difficulties prevent them from seeking help.
    - Address safeguarding concerns that arise from interactions. SEMH and safeguarding often overlap in complex ways.

What to watch for

Escalating anxiety, school avoidance (which can look like illness, stomach aches or 'I forgot my PE kit again'), home-school communication breakdown, safeguarding concerns, impact on other students, and staff wellbeing.

Visual impairment

Students with visual impairments range from having low vision to total blindness, so each student has unique visual needs. This is an area where you absolutely must work with specialist – even if the VI is not severe, a specialist assessment and recommendation is crucial.

What's different for visual impairment

- **Specialist involvement is best practice:**
    - Secure qualified teachers of the visually impaired (QTVIs) and implement their recommendations precisely.
    - Work with the RNIB for resources as they have materials and expertise you won't find elsewhere.
- **Materials need specific adaptations:**
    - Provide large print, but not just 'bigger' content; specific font sizes matter, as recommended by your QTVI. Provide Braille resources where needed.
    - RNIB offers exam and classwork services. If a student uses Braille, they need Braille materials, not just audio. Ensure high contrast, like black on white or yellow; as per recommendations for individual students.
    - Make all digital content compatible with screen readers. If your PowerPoint doesn't work with a screen reader, search for a 'work around'.
- **Assistive technology is essential:**
    - Provide screen readers and magnification software like ZoomText. NVDA (Nonvisual Desktop Access) is an example of a free, open-source Windows screen reader.
    - Provide electronic note-takers like BrailleNote or accessible iPads.
    - Ensure text-to-speech availability, which should already be part of your adaption toolkit.

- **Teaching adaptations are essential:**
  - Ask your VI team to support with verbalising visual content training.
  - Provide pre-reading materials in accessible formats to give students time to prepare.
  - Use tactile resources – raised maps, 3D models, textured materials. Let students feel what they can't see.
  - Ensure PE staff are specifically trained. VI students can participate in PE; they just need appropriate adaptations.
- **Mobility support matters:**
  - Support use of mobility aids – canes, guide dogs. Support children if they are self-concious about using these adaptions.
  - Maintain consistent layouts – stop rearranging furniture. Mark edges clearly with high-contrast tape.
  - Train all staff and peers in respectful interaction with mobility aids.

What to watch for

Check that equipment is functioning as intended (for example, is the screen reader actually working). Ensure staff are consistently verbalising key visual information; this is something learning walks will highlight.

Confirm that materials are available in the correct format at the right time, not delayed. Also consider how safely pupils are able to navigate the school environment day to day.

Hearing impairment

Students with hearing impairments range from mild to profound hearing loss and may use hearing aids, cochlear implants, or British Sign Language (BSL). Like visual impairment, this absolutely requires specialist input.

What's different for hearing impairment

- **Specialist involvement is mandatory:**
  - Secure teachers of the deaf (ToDs) and implement their recommendations precisely.
  - Coordinate with audiologists for equipment checks because if hearing aids aren't working properly, everything else is pointless.

- For students who use British Sign Language (BSL) or other forms of communication, ensure they have access to a communication support worker or an interpreter.

- **Acoustic environment is critical:**
  - Audit classroom acoustics. Hard surfaces bounce sound around, which is awful for students with HI. Minimise echo through absorbent surfaces, lower ceilings where possible.
  - Implement sound amplification systems – radio aids, hearing loops.
  - Position students away from noisy equipment.
  - Keep doors and windows closed to reduce background noise.
- **Seating is considered:**
  - Position students where they can see teacher and classmates. Often this is the front, but not always – ask them what works.
  - Keep students away from noisy areas like windows, doors, high-traffic zones.
  - Use U-shaped seating for group discussions so students can see everyone who's speaking.
  - Ensure your face is well-lit when speaking.
- **Communication needs specific training:**
  - Train staff to face students when speaking.
  - Use clear speech at moderate pace. Don't shout (it distorts sound) or over-exaggerate (it distorts lip patterns).
  - Ensure all videos are subtitled. If they're not, find different videos or make transcripts.
  - Repeat and rephrase in group discussions. Following multiple speakers is genuinely difficult.
  - Support peers in learning communication strategies. All students can learn to be more inclusive.
- **Extracurricular inclusion matters:**
  - Make adjustments for all activities – PE, sports, clubs.
  - Use radio aids where appropriate during activities. Technology works everywhere, not just in classrooms.
  - Train all staff including playground monitors and lunchtime supervisors.

What to watch for

Equipment functioning (dead batteries in hearing aids are a constant issue), acoustic quality of spaces, subtitles actually available and working, student able to follow discussions in class.

Physical difficulties (PD)

There's such a vast array of different physical needs that trying to generalise is almost pointless. Each student requires individual assessment, and you need medical information and professional input to get this right.

What's different for physical difficulties

- **Planning and risk assessment are crucial:**
  - Complete comprehensive risk assessments for all activities.
  - Develop care plans that everyone can follow.
  - Plan carefully for school trips, PE lessons, movement between classes.
  - Build adequate time into timetables because rushing with mobility difficulties is both unsupportive and potentially dangerous.
  - Consider energy and fatigue in your planning. Moving is exhausting for students with PD; factor this into expectations.
- **Equipment and adaptations:**
  - Consult the student's occupational therapist (OT) or specilaist teacher about seating and equipment. Monitor equipment adjustments as students grow because growth spurts happen fast and equipment needs frequent adjusting.
  - Request specialist technology assessments when you need expert advice. Work closely with occupational therapists on their recommendations. OTs are brilliant; use their expertise.
- **Inclusion in all activities:**
  - Ensure participation in PE, swimming, break time. Don't just exempt students with PD from everything physical. Adapt activities, don't exclude from them.
  - Plan carefully with student input because they know what they can and can't do.

- Support social and emotional wellbeing. Being physically different is emotionally challenging, and this needs acknowledging and supporting.

- **Student voice and peer education:**
  - Allow students to present their needs to their class if they want to. Some want to explain, some don't. Plan this carefully with the student. Make it empowering, not embarrassing.
  - Teach acceptance and inclusion to all pupils. Educate peers, don't just hope for kindness. Address the fact that feeling 'different' is hard. Acknowledge it, don't dismiss it.
- **Multi-agency coordination matters:**
  - Work with OTs, school nurses, physiotherapists, families. That's a lot of professionals, so coordinate effectively. Streamline meetings to save everyone's time – combine IEP meetings, TAF meetings, OT visits where possible.
  - Seek parental insight regularly. Keep communication open because needs change and you need to stay informed.

What to watch for

Equipment functioning and fitting correctly (equipment that doesn't fit properly is worse), fatigue levels (are expectations realistic?), social inclusion (are they actually included or just present?), adjustments clearly being made.

Speech, Language and Communication Needs (SLCN)

In areas of social disadvantage, very high proportions of children may start school with delayed language development, with national estimates suggesting around one in five children begin school without the language skills they need for learning (Speech and Language UK, 2023). This affects everything else because language underpins all learning. The good news is that this is often the easiest fix in Early Years if addressed promptly with no other co-existing needs. Sometimes it's genuinely just that students haven't been exposed to a wide vocabulary at home or have limited experience visiting places such as beaches, zoos or farms, and targeted intervention can help them make rapid progress.

Understanding the presentation

Students with SLCN have difficulties with understanding language, expressing themselves, or social communication. This isn't about accent or dialect – it's about fundamental language processing. Some students can't understand what's being said to them. Some can't find the words to express what they're thinking. Some understand and can speak but can't navigate the social rules of communication.

What's different for SLCN beyond the universal

- **Language-rich environment is intensified:**
  - Make communication the absolute priority across your school. Language underpins everything – reading, writing, maths, science, social interaction, emotional regulation, everything. Display vocabulary, sentence starters, word banks everywhere. Make language visible.
  - Pre-teach subject-specific vocabulary systematically. Don't assume students know the words.
  - Use choices of alternatives rather than open-ended questions where helpful, e.g. 'Pen or pencil?' not 'What do you want?'. Incorporate dual coding in everything. Words and pictures make for better understanding for everyone.
- **SLCN-specific strategies matter:**
  - Break instructions into very simple steps.
  - Model correct sentence structures rather than correcting directly; 'Yes, the dog is running' not 'No, say it properly.'
  - Use expansion techniques. If a child says 'Dog,' you say 'Yes, the dog is running.' You're building on what they said, not correcting it.
  - Provide structured communication opportunities because some students need practice in safe settings.
  - Implement listening activities and phonological awareness games. Sound awareness comes before reading.
- **Staff training is specialised:**
  - Make SLCN support whole-staff responsibility, not just the SENDCo's job. Everyone communicates with students experiencing SLCN needs.
  - Provide ongoing CPD in communication-friendly strategies. This is skills-building, not one-off awareness.
  - Create a culture of shared expertise with speech and language therapists. Bridge the gap between specialist advice and classroom practice.

    - Train LSAs to deliver targeted interventions. Upskill your team to deliver interventions in between SaLT visits.

- **Speech and Language Therapy partnership:**
    - Build strong relationships with SaLTs. Consider commissioning your own SaLT to visit once per half term. Sometimes buying capacity beats waiting for NHS provision, which can be highly variable.
    - Implement SaLT recommendations consistently.
    - Bridge the gap between specialist advice and classroom practice. Make sure advice is actually usable for your staff.

- **Social communication support:**
    - Explicitly teach social communication skills for key students.
    - Teachers can also use social stories to help students understand expected behaviours in different situations.
    - For example, 'It's raining cats and dogs' needs explaining, not assumed understanding.
    - Pair students with good peer role models for communication, but structure this properly.

- **Early intervention focus:**
    - Screen for SLCN at school entry both at primary and secondary – many children in primary have been missed and labelled as SEMH incorrectly. Catch difficulties early. Provide focused intervention immediately. Don't wait months while you observe or wait for formal diagnosis.
    - Recognise that early intervention for SLCN often shows rapid progress. Sometimes this genuinely is the quickest fix.

What to watch for

Language development progress, social interaction quality, vocabulary growth, implementation of SaLT recommendations.

Pathological Demand Avoidance and Oppositional Defiant Disorder

Both need handling extremely carefully. Educators can't diagnose these conditions, and attempting to do so is both above our expertise and potentially harmful. However, understanding the differences can help you support students more effectively while you wait for proper assessment.

Understanding the differences

- Pathological Demand Avoidance (PDA) is part of the autism spectrum and is driven by extreme anxiety. Students avoid everyday demands because they feel overwhelmed and out of control. It's not about being challenging for the sake of it; it's about managing unbearable anxiety. They may appear to agree with requests but then find ways to avoid actually doing them. It's subtle.
- Oppositional Defiant Disorder (ODD) is a behavioural disorder where defiance is more deliberate and driven by anger, frustration or a sense of unfairness. It's direct: arguing back, refusing outright, doing the opposite of what's asked.

What's different with PDA and ODD

- **Train staff in differences:**
  - Ensure all staff understand the fundamental difference: PDA is anxiety-driven demand avoidance; ODD is anger-driven defiance. Focus on what drives the behaviour, not just what it looks like.
  - Recognise different triggers: anxiety for PDA, frustration/unfairness for ODD.
  - Never allow casual diagnosis from your staff. We describe behaviours; we don't diagnose.
- **PDA-specific approach:**
  - Implement low-demand approaches. Reduce anxiety by giving genuine choice. Offer choices rather than direct demands.
  - Use gentle suggestions and indirect requests. 'I wonder if...' works better than 'You need to...'.
  - Provide flexibility and understanding. Reduce the overall demand load systematically.
- **ODD-specific approach:**
  - Maintain clear boundaries and consistency. Ensure students know rules and consequences.
  - Provide plenty of praise for compliance.
  - Be fair and transparent in all dealings. These students have often experienced unfairness; don't add to it.

- **Support their families:**
    - Help families understand the differences without labelling their child.
    - Describe specific behaviours you're seeing.
    - Provide consistent approaches between home and school.
    - Access appropriate specialist support for proper assessment and diagnosis.

What to watch for

Anxiety levels, response to different types of demands, behavioural patterns, family stress levels.

Positive handling: a critical leadership responsibility

Positive handling (formerly referred to as 'restraint'), is an understandably contentious issue in schools, and one that requires careful consideration. While it's sometimes necessary to prevent students from harming themselves or others, getting it right can be a challenge and getting it wrong can lead to serious legal and professional consequences.

Understanding your legal position

The Education and Inspections Act 2006 gives school staff legal power to use reasonable force to prevent students from committing criminal offenses, causing injury to themselves or others, damaging property or disrupting good order and discipline. The Children and Families Act 2014 emphasises protecting vulnerable children, including those with SEND. Force must only be used as a last resort and must be proportionate and reasonable – the minimum necessary to achieve the desired result.

Protecting everyone involved

Never expect untrained staff to deal with complex situations involving potential physical intervention. This is unfair to staff and unsafe for students. Provide comprehensive training to all staff, not just those working with challenging behaviour. You never know who'll end up in a situation requiring positive handling. Complete risk assessments for students who may need physical intervention to protect staff from potential lawsuits and protect students from inappropriate interventions.

SEND considerations are critical

Make reasonable adjustments before using physical intervention. Use specialist de-escalation techniques appropriate for the student's needs. Ensure staff are trained in handling students with specific conditions – autism, ADHD, sensory processing difficulties all require different approaches. Recognise that failure to make reasonable adjustments may be discrimination under the Equality Act 2010, which can lead to legal challenges.

Systems and recording

Develop a clear written policy on use of reasonable force. Record all incidents in detail – what led to it, what force was used, what the outcome was. These records are crucial if there are ever complaints or legal proceedings. Inform parents whenever physical intervention is used. Explain why it was necessary and what steps you're taking to prevent it being needed again. Review incidents systematically to identify patterns and improve practice.

Be prepared

Even if you don't currently have students requiring positive handling, train all staff anyway. Be ready for all eventualities. Recognise that dysregulation and challenging behaviour are becoming more common. Don't wait until crisis to implement systems. Staff deserve training and protection. Students deserve safe, appropriate support.

What to watch for

Incidents requiring positive handling, staff confidence levels, quality of parental communication, policy adherence, patterns suggesting prevention strategies aren't working.

Labels and diagnosis

Let's address something that comes up constantly: the obsession with labels. Labels can be helpful for understanding needs and accessing support, but they can also trap us into thinking that without a diagnosis, nothing can be done.

Many children don't meet diagnostic thresholds or face years-long waits for assessments, but they still have real, immediate needs that require support now.

Creating culture change

Make absolutely clear that in your school, support is based on need, not labels. Put reasonable adjustments in place without waiting for formal diagnosis. Challenge staff who say 'we can't do anything without a diagnosis.' That's not true, and it's not acceptable. Focus on 'what can we do right now to help this child?'

Recognise current assessment delays. Some waits are literally years. Don't let lack of a label become an excuse for lack of support. Implement the Graduated Approach regardless of diagnosis. Describe behaviours and needs you're seeing; provide support based on those observations.

Preventing informal diagnosis

Never allow staff to suggest specific diagnoses to parents. Even with expertise, this isn't our role and can cause significant harm. I learned this the hard way about 15 years ago when I suggested ASD to a student's carers. A complaint was lodged because I was unaware at the time how responses to trauma and ASD traits can overlap.

When we hint at a diagnosis, we might inadvertently raise concerns or expectations that aren't helpful. Conditions and trauma responses can overlap in confusing ways. Stick to facts: 'We've noticed these specific behaviours.' Guide parents toward seeking help: 'Your child seems to be struggling with X, Y, and Z. It might be helpful to explore this further with a professional.' Maintain professional boundaries.

The bottom line

Teaching is about seeing the child in front of you, not just the paperwork. Create a school culture where staff are empowered to support all children based on their observed needs, while maintaining appropriate professional boundaries around diagnosis. Fair doesn't mean identical; fair means everyone gets what they need to succeed.

The most effective schools don't create separate systems for each condition. They build one strong, flexible, inclusive system (those universal pillars) and then make informed adjustments for specific needs. This is more efficient, more consistent, and ultimately more inclusive than trying to run parallel systems for different diagnoses. It's also more sustainable when your staff are already stretched.

This section was a snapshot into the first steps in supporting a variety of needs, children don't fit into neat boxes, so always respond to individual need, seek and take on board professional recommendations.

The next chapters will build on this foundation, showing you how to implement whole-school strategies that make inclusion a reality rather than just an aspiration. Because at the end of the day, that's what we're all here for – helping every child access learning and belong in our schools.

Part 2

Whole-school strategies

9 Pulling together: making inclusion work

When it comes to inclusion, you'll be relieved to know that the key isn't always found in expensive interventions, glossy schemes or a pie-in-the-sky increase in the budget. It lies in the collective mindset of your school community: what you believe about children, what you prioritise and how well you work together. This isn't about expensive interventions or waiting for more funding. The most powerful inclusive practices are often the simplest – and many cost nothing at all.

The power of a whole-school approach

It's easy to assume that SEND is mainly the SENDCo's responsibility. In reality, the SEND Code of Practice (2015) makes it clear that every teacher has a role in meeting children's additional needs – and, by extension, every leader does too. Inclusion only works when the whole school shares the responsibility. It relies on a common understanding and a consistent way of talking about and supporting children, not on one person trying to lead the charge alone.

When every staff member is on the same page, we create consistency. Children learn what to expect and staff feel confident in how to respond. There's nothing quite as powerful as a school where everyone plays a part in supporting every learner.

A whole-school strategy isn't about uniformity for its own sake, which can be divisive. It's about cohesion. Consistent routines, visuals, expectations and language around additional needs help prevent the 'luck of the draw' experience some children face when moving between classrooms. Of course, staff bring different strengths and areas for development, and in the current recruitment and retention climate I know that it isn't always as easy as I'm making it out to be.

Empathy for the realities of school life

No strategy will succeed without recognising the pressures staff are under. Budgets are tighter than ever. LSAs are stretched. Teachers are supporting more than thirty unique learners while navigating a curriculum that doesn't pause for anyone. Personally, I miss the more laid-back days before the 2014 curriculum reforms.

So, when we talk about improving inclusive practice, it has to come with empathy. Staff need support, not guilt trips; encouragement, not non-negotiable checklists of tasks to complete. If you really want colleagues to try something new or reflect on their practice, you need to begin from a place of trust and understanding.

Small shifts and marginal gains are more sustainable than sweeping overhauls, even when the challenges feel huge. Time-efficient tweaks are easier to adopt. It can be tempting to go in all guns blazing when the issues and solutions seem obvious and you want everything fixed now, but long-term change needs a gentler approach – more taming a scared cat than a bull in a china shop. That slower, more patient method is far more likely to win hearts and minds (and the odd treat doesn't hurt). Often, a genuine 'thank you' and a cup of tea do more for school culture than expensive external CPD.

SENDCos belong at the decision-making table

For SEND to be prioritised, SENDCos must be strategically involved. That means being an active part of discussions about curriculum, staffing, behaviour policies, CPD and resourcing – not simply being consulted once decisions have already been made.

Too often, SENDCos are expected to deliver big results with minimal involvement in the processes that shape provision. Any sentence in an inspection report that mentions SEND is, to the outside world at least, automatically viewed as the SENDCo's responsibility, even when they have little to no influence over staffing or structures.

I've seen this first hand: being held accountable for provision decisions I had no say in. It's frustrating and, frankly, unfair. But it illustrates a wider point: the SENDCo's role needs to continue shifting. It is best practice for the SENDCo to be part of the SLT, able to contribute meaningfully to discussions around teaching and learning, student progress and staffing. When the SENDCo's voice is central to school improvement planning, the impact on inclusion is tangible. Schools move from reactive firefighting to proactive, sustainable development.

This doesn't mean every SENDCo must sit on the senior leadership team. In some schools the system works well without that, as long as the SENDCo's voice is genuinely heard. When I moved from assistant headship into a SENDCo role, it made sense for me to be part of the leadership team – I had whole-school improvement experience and my skills were used well.

But it's also worth considering what your SLT membership actually looks like. If the SENDCo is expected to attend SLT meetings, think about whether they need to be there for the full meeting or whether SEND could be discussed early, allowing them time to focus on the many other demands of the role. Personally, I was happy to stay for the whole meeting. My current school is different: I'm not on the leadership team, but as we're a tiny school and I'm only there one day a week, the system works. We have a head of school and an executive headteacher, and communication is strong.

Everyone, every day

Let's return to whole-school approaches. Improving inclusion isn't about grand gestures; it's about building a culture. It's shaped by what we do daily – how we greet children, how we adapt without fuss, how we talk about need, how we listen and how we build positive relationships. When everyone understands their role in inclusion, and when those roles are respected and properly resourced (starting with time and empathy), the small, everyday actions begin to join up. Over time, those marginal gains create meaningful, long-term culture shifts.

Progress may feel slow, and you might not see big changes day to day, but when you look back after a term or two, you can be proud of how far you've come and what has been achieved.

10 Whole-school mindset: gratitude, kindness and inclusive attitudes

If you've ever tried to change the culture of a school by introducing yet another initiative, you'll know it often lands with the collective enthusiasm of a teacher who's just had their PPA cancelled. The truth is, sustainable change isn't about quick wins or launching new initiatives constantly; it's about embedding a mindset across your school that values kindness, inclusivity and a genuine belief that all children (and adults) can thrive with the right support.

A culture of kindness is an intentional and powerful act of choosing empathy over judgement every single day. In inclusive schools, kindness is built into the daily habits of everyone: staff, children and leadership. It sits in how we speak to each other, how we respond to behaviour and how we manage mistakes (including our own).

Some schools have done this brilliantly. John Magee's *Kindness Matters* approach (2020), for example, has been adopted by many schools committed to embedding kindness into their culture. Research on kindness-focused programmes more broadly shows promising outcomes: when kindness is prioritised in schools, there are improvements in school climate and safety, reductions in bullying and negative behaviours, and increased attendance and student wellbeing (Datu et al., 2022; Kaplan et al., 2016; Mental Health Foundation, 2020). Children want to be there, and so do the staff.

Where does gratitude come in?

If kindness is the ethos, gratitude is the engine. Gratitude, especially when modelled by senior leaders, builds trust and positivity. A regular 'thank you', staff genuinely feeling appreciated, or a moment of quiet acknowledgement can go a long way in maintaining morale, particularly in environments where demands are high and budgets are tight.

Cultivating a culture of gratitude with students can also support emotional resilience, reduce anxiety and develop belonging. Try five-minute gratitude journals in tutor time, end-of-day reflection activities or even a classroom gratitude wall. It sounds small but it's not a waste of learning time. These moments become the habits that build emotionally literate, reflective humans. I love a marginal gain that joins with others to make big, sustained changes!

What does an inclusive attitude look like?

It's easy to say 'we're inclusive'. The acid test is in the everyday decisions – how we timetable, who gets to go on the trip, whether we really believe that a pre-verbal child deserves a part in the school play. Inclusivity isn't about surface-level stuff; it's about who's welcome in your community and what you're willing to adapt to make that possible.

Your leadership is central here. If you, as a senior leader, approach SEND, EAL, SEMH and other additional needs as bolt-ons or barriers, that mindset *will* trickle down. But if you genuinely see difference as a strength and support staff to do the same, the whole climate shifts. Once inclusion is seen as everyone's responsibility, you've got a solid foundation. It's not about being perfect, it's about being intentional. If your school gets this bit right, the rest (your interventions, your wellbeing offer, your universal provision) will have strong foundations to build on.

Reflection questions

- **What acts of kindness are embedded into your systems rather than left to chance?**
- **How do you demonstrate gratitude, and how often do you encourage others to do the same?**
- **Do all students, regardless of need or background, have equitable access to opportunity, challenge and celebration?**

11 Whole-school universal provision

If you're relying solely on interventions to meet the needs of your students with SEND, it's a bit like using a colander to carry soup. Some will get through, but the system itself isn't built to hold it all. That's where universal provision comes in: it's your whole-school, every day, 'no-extra-paperwork-required' offer for all children. It should be so embedded that you'd struggle to point to where 'inclusion' starts and ends, because it's just how you do things.

Universal provision is *not* about lowering expectations. It's about creating the conditions where every child can access good or better teaching, right from the start. For leaders, this means working with your SENDCo and senior leaders to define: 'What do we expect to see in every classroom, for every child, every day?'.

Co-defining your universal offer

The first step is clarity. Too often, universal provision is a nebulous concept in a school policy, well-meaning but vague, especially as there are various terms for the same thing, such as 'Tier 1 support' or 'ordinarily available'. So, gather your whole staff and co-create a list of agreed whole-school practices. This should include the strategies we discussed in Chapter 7: adaptive teaching, scaffolding, dual coding, wait time, etc.. Your job as a leader is to move them from 'good ideas some teachers use' to 'non-negotiables everyone uses'.

This list then becomes your school's baseline for inclusion. The Education Endowment Foundation's 'Five a Day' adaptive teaching strategies are a good place to start (EEF, 2021). Your LA may have their own universal provision support materials as well.

Top Tip

It's worth looking at various LA websites to find resources for universal provision that can work for your school if your LA's resources are lacking.

Why this matters

Getting universal provision right means you're already addressing many of the specific needs we explored in Chapter 8. You're not waiting to identify a need and then scramble to adapt, you're embedding inclusion from the start.

When your universal provision is strong, it becomes clearer who genuinely needs additional layers of support because the groundwork has already been done. It may even lead to a reduction in your register as children are able to cope more effectively in class and therefore able to access the curriculum more easily. You'll also be able to spot needs earlier, because when your school's classroom expectations are consistent and supportive, a child who still struggles stands out more clearly and signals the need for further investigation. Universal strategies don't just benefit students with SEND. Everyone benefits from structure, clarity, positive relationships and a calm classroom climate. That's what makes it good teaching.

Supporting your teachers when they need backup

The layer above the classroom also needs careful consideration:

- What happens when a concern arises in class?
- Is there someone always available to support?
- What does this structure look like?
- Is the provided support documented?
- Does everyone understand next steps?
- Is there shared language?
- Does it fit well with your school behaviour policy? (See Chapter 12 for SEMH support structures).
- Are there different considerations for individual children?

Even excellent teachers struggle without confidence in the support structure above them, whether that's senior leaders, pastoral LSAs, the SENDCo or your inclusion team. In schools with high levels of need, this scaffolding for staff is imperative. (We'll explore the SENDCo's role in this support structure in Part 3.)

If you've inherited a school where teaching and learning is of concern, moving to good or better feels daunting. It's entirely possible, but it requires small manageable steps, a team willing to work toward a shared goal, and clarity about what inclusion actually looks like in practice (which is why Chapter 9's work on whole-school mindset matters so much).

Your responsibilities

There are several key aspects to consider here:

- **Auditing:** Walk your school with your SENDCo. Are the agreed-upon strategies visible in every classroom? If not, why not? There's no need to name and shame, just keep embedding them as best practice, and ask questions.
- **Training:** Make sure CPD includes regular revisits to universal strategies, with opportunities for modelling, sharing practice and peer observation, as well as key training such as SLCN classroom strategies.
- **Planning:** Work with your SENDCo to ensure teaching staff aren't constantly reinventing the wheel. Build inclusive strategies into curriculum planning, not just behaviour policies. Make it as easy as possible for staff by ensuring visual supports like 'now and next' boards are readily available. You might ask your LSA team to create scaffolding packs for every classroom during an INSET day. Decide what you want to see at the planning stage to support children with additional needs (e.g. using the notes section in PowerPoint).
- **Resources:** Many counties have detailed information on universally available tiered provision. Investigate what's out there and use one as a baseline for your CPD and expectations. I use Essex's resources, which are pretty comprehensive.
- **Celebrate:** When a teacher adapts brilliantly, when an LSA spots a clever scaffold that works, when a class becomes more inclusive just by embedding one small change. These achievements can become harder to spot once they're seamless, so look carefully!

When you get universal provision right, the phrase 'we're an inclusive school' moves from aspiration to observable practice.

Universal design for learning (UDL)

This is an educational framework designed to make learning accessible and an approach used to deliver universal provision. It recognises that learners process information and engage with content in different ways. It's rooted in neuroscience and aims to create flexible learning environments that remove barriers before they come up, rather than relying solely on individual accommodations after difficulties appear (CAST, 2018).

UDL is built around three core principles:

1. **multiple means of engagement** – how students get motivated and stay involved (the why of learning)
2. **multiple means of representation** – how students access and understand information (the what)
3. **multiple means of action and expression** – how students demonstrate what they know (the how).

The goal is to design lessons, activities and assessments that provide various pathways so all learners – including those with SEND, EAL or different learning preferences – can succeed without unnecessary barriers.

What UDL can do for your school

At its heart, UDL is about proactive inclusion, not reactive scrambling. Instead of waiting for a student to struggle and then adapting on the fly, you're championing curriculum design that anticipates diverse needs from the outset. This reduces exclusions, behaviour issues and disengagement – and it aligns with what Ofsted and the SEND Code of Practice (2015) expect: high-quality, inclusive teaching as the foundation, not a bolt-on intervention.

There's also a workload benefit. When flexible approaches are built into everyday practice, teachers spend less time retrofitting individual adjustments and more time delivering lessons that work for everyone. However, this doesn't happen by accident. It requires whole-school buy-in and ongoing CPD – not a one-off training, but a culture shift.

Finally, UDL enhances student agency. When students have choice and autonomy in how they learn and demonstrate understanding, motivation and self-regulation improve; skills that matter far beyond school.

How to embed UDL

- Champion UDL as part of your school's vision for inclusion. Make it clear it's everyone's business, not just for SEND or inclusion teams.
- Invest in training and resources to help staff understand and apply UDL principles across subjects and year groups.
- Ensure curriculum planning time includes thinking about varied means of engagement, representation and expression, not just content coverage.
- Embed UDL in policies and lesson observations as a marker of best-quality teaching and inclusive practice.
- Encourage collaboration across departments and with students to co-design learning experiences that reflect different needs.
- Celebrate examples where UDL makes a real difference to students' engagement and progress.

The beauty of UDL is that *it works*. It reduces teacher workload, improves outcomes for all students, and makes inclusion the default rather than something you retrofit. Get it right, and your UP will do a lot of heavy lifting.

Equal opportunities for extracurricular activities

The school experience doesn't begin and end with the bell. For many students, the magic happens outside the standard timetable: football, choir, chess, drama, robotics. These are the spaces where confidence grows, friendships deepen and students discover what lights them up. So, it's vital that everyone, including pupils with SEND, has the opportunity to participate.

Often, exclusion isn't deliberate but logistical. A child needs 1:1 support at lunchtime to access a club, but the LSA is elsewhere. A parent can't stay after school so the child with medical needs doesn't attend. A student with anxiety or sensory processing difficulties finds the noise overwhelming and avoids joining altogether.

Unless you're actively looking, you won't spot who isn't attending, and why. Do a quiet audit. Speak to your students and their families. Check your attendance lists against your SEND register and other vulnerable groups. The gap is often wider than you think.

Make it possible, not just available

Once you know who's missing out, the next question is: what do we need to put in place to make it possible for them to join in? That might include:

- providing 1:1 or additional support during clubs for students with EHCPs or high needs
- adjusting activities to be more inclusive (e.g. visual prompts in chess club, sensory-friendly adaptations in drama)
- using Pupil Premium or EHCP funding creatively to support club attendance
- supporting transitions into clubs by offering taster sessions, buddy systems or parental visits
- training club leaders and external providers on SEND-aware approaches.

Sometimes it's small, thoughtful amendments that make the biggest difference.

Shared responsibility and systematising access

Again, this isn't a job for the SENDCo. Inclusion in extracurricular activities should sit across leadership, with clubs treated as part of the curriculum experience. Ensure there's a clear process for identifying what support students need and who is responsible for putting it in place. That might mean looking at staffing rotas or asking LSAs if they'd like to run (and be paid for) a club themselves. If you're in a multi-academy trust, you might be able to collaborate across schools to offer joint clubs or shared provision for students with similar needs. The more flexible and creative you can be, the more likely you are to reach the students who need it most.

Ultimately, extracurricular provision is about belonging. A student who joins a club and is successful in that context often carries that confidence back into the classroom (see Chapter 13 for more on how belonging impacts attendance).

I used to run a school club called 'Golden Group'. We did a different activity each week involving craft, cooking, forest schools: all focused on speaking, listening and social skills. The students, who were very quiet in school, blossomed and became much more confident. Golden Group was by invitation, specifically designed for children who weren't drawn to mainstream clubs.

This kind of targeted provision can be a protected factor for wellbeing, a motivator for attendance (see Chapter 13) and, for some, the difference between just surviving school and really connecting with it. If your vision is truly inclusive, it has to stretch beyond lesson time.

12 Supporting SEMH across the school

In Chapter 8, we explored the most common areas of SEND you'll encounter in your school. This chapter shows you how to embed whole-school support for those needs – particularly SEMH, SLCN and literacy difficulties – through structures, strategies and leadership that go beyond individual classroom practice. Think of this as moving from knowing what the needs are to building the systems that support them.

You're probably familiar with this scenario: a student is really struggling and showing emotional dysregulation, with big behaviours (communication) or retreating into shutdown mode. It may not be just one but several at the same time! The referral process makes you feel like you're failing the student. CAMHS is overwhelmed, your local behaviour support team has a six-month waiting list, and there's no one available to carry out an assessment any time soon.

In the meantime, your school still needs to support that student every day, and their teachers too (or work to reintegrate the student if they are school-avoiding). Staff are already doing their best to manage with limited resources and a great deal of goodwill. *That's* why having a clear in-house structure for supporting SEMH is absolutely vital. It's not about replacing external services, it's about filling the gap with something meaningful while you wait.

What does an effective SEMH structure look like?

It starts with a graduated approach (see Chapter 7) for all emotional and behavioural needs. The 'wait and see' model is a disservice to both children and staff. Every school needs a tiered system of support: universal strategies for all (Chapter 11), targeted interventions for those at risk and more intensive, personalised support for those with ongoing needs.

This shouldn't be left to chance or just added to the SENDCo's list. In a larger school, it's worth having both a behaviour and a pastoral lead who can meet regularly with the SENDCo to discuss joined-up approaches. I worked in a large school using this model and quickly discovered there were students with persistently challenging behaviour who I knew nothing about. They were quickly added to my SEND register for SEMH and further investigation (raising my register by ten per cent – but needs must).

Significant SEMH needs often stem from root causes that could have been supported sooner if we weren't all so stretched. A student may have experienced adverse childhood experiences (ACEs), have underlying SEND such as neurodiversity, or present with unidentified speech, language and communication needs. Many students are never screened for SLCN at primary school and their limited language skills can show up as frustration or disengagement. It's essential to screen and address SLCN on entry to primary school, and, as this doesn't always happen, to screen again in Year 7.

Creating clear pathways of referral

Create a clear referral pathway within school. Set out which behaviours or needs trigger extra support and record them in an annotatable support plan (you might call it a 'consistent support plan'). This can sit alongside or replace an IEP and should spell out what support looks like – access to a learning mentor, regular check-ins with an LSA trained in emotional coaching, or a space to regulate before returning to class. Put it on paper, and make sure everyone knows what's available and how to access it. Students move between many different adults during the day, so everyone needs to understand the process to keep things consistent. (There are some children whose needs are so bespoke that they require high-needs support. In these cases, request an EHCP assessment at the earliest opportunity.)

This includes emotionally based school avoiders – we no longer say 'school refuser', as avoidance is anxiety-driven (see Chapter 13 for more). In these situations, flexibility is essential. We don't want a plethora of reduced timetables, but, when used appropriately, they can be a tool for reintegration rather than exclusion. Make sure these are always planned with a clear goal in mind and reviewed regularly. When considering a part-time timetable, there is usually LA paperwork to complete.

When to refer externally

There's no exact science, but a good rule of thumb is that when a student's needs are beyond your current provision and there's evidence of this over time, you should ask for help. Remember that wait times are long, so it's a good idea to refer at the earliest opportunity.

Unfortunately, schools also find themselves in situations where there is high need but external services don't agree. This is where tools like Boxall Profiles

(Bennathan and Boxall, 1998), targeted SEMH interventions, and emotional literacy groups come into their own. Consider investing in school counsellors or a play therapist (if funds allow). At the very least, an LSA with some basic pastoral training is a good starting point.

Train your whole staff in emotionally intelligent approaches – emotion coaching, restorative conversations and low-arousal responses. SEMH support needs to be part of whole-school pedagogy.

Getting started: your SEMH audit

- **Map your offer.** What SEMH support do you already have? Who delivers it? Who can access it? Write it down and make it visible.
- **Train staff.** Everyone from midday supervisors to SLT needs a basic toolkit for emotional regulation and trauma-informed practice.
- **Normalise regulation.** Having a wobble shouldn't feel like failure. Build a culture where students learn that dysregulation is something we can work through, not something that's punished.
- **Work with families.** Especially for school-avoiding children, a partnership with parents is essential. Even small wins – an hour a day, a virtual check-in – can rebuild bridges.

If we don't provide safety, consistency and emotional containment in school, where else are these children going to get it? I was talking with a SENDCo recently about a student who went from throwing chairs regularly to being a full part of his class. This was down to the hard work and dedication of everyone involved and included school therapeutic interventions with a specialist they employed. When schools are able to dedicate resources to give individuals the best chance possible, you can achieve a lot – albeit in tiny steps.

An SEMH-informed curriculum and explicit mental health teaching

Emotional regulation used to be sort of left to chance; something students were expected to just pick up along the way. Now, schools are increasingly filling in the gaps, and even more children need support in this area. SEMH needs don't exist in a vacuum that's addressed briefly with a weekly PSHE lesson. It's crucial that SEMH is built in, not bolted on.

What does an SEMH-informed curriculum look like?

An SEMH-informed curriculum embeds emotional literacy, regulation strategies and mental health awareness across subjects and key stages as part of everyday teaching and learning, not just in PSHE. It teaches children how to 'be' in the world, how to relate to others and how to manage themselves.

Key elements of a good SEMH-informed curriculum include:

- **explicit teaching of emotional language**, giving children the vocabulary to describe their feelings accurately from the EYFS upwards
- **regular opportunities for reflection and discussion**, such as circle time, journaling or guided group work
- **mindfulness and calming activities** as part of the school week, for everyone, not just 'troubled' students
- **sequenced content around wellbeing** and mental health in PSHE, RSE and form time
- **opportunities to support students** when issues arise, such as through learning mentors and pastoral support
- **staff modelling** of emotionally healthy behaviours.

Whenever I train staff on attachment theory, I always include a disclaimer that some colleagues may find themselves reflecting on their own upbringing and may wish to seek further support afterwards.[1] There's also a lot to be said for developing staff's emotional resilience; we can probably all think of times when we could have responded in a more emotionally mature way.

Making SEMH teaching meaningful

SEMH teaching needs to be responsive to student needs and embedded in whole-school practice. Are your teachers confident talking about mental health? Do they seek support for themselves? Are your behaviour policies aligned with your SEMH approach? If not, start there. Some schools go further by creating dedicated wellbeing sessions in the timetable or adopting trauma-informed curricula that explicitly centre relationship-building and emotional regulation.

Again, don't leave this work solely to your pastoral lead or SENDCo. A genuinely SEMH-informed curriculum requires everyone to be involved. It is the

[1] *Attachment theory* refers to the way early relationships with primary caregivers shape a child's sense of safety, emotional regulation and ability to form secure relationships. These discussions can surface personal memories or reflections for staff, so it's important to acknowledge this and signpost support if needed.

cumulative impact of many small, daily interactions that helps a child feel seen, safe and understood. Train your staff and trust them. Some of the most effective work in this area comes from casual conversations at breaktime or from the mentor who sits beside a child at breakfast club.

Assessing impact

There is no need to measure wellbeing in neat data points. Look at engagement; ask children what they're learning. Use simple tools such as student voice or wellbeing surveys. Ofsted will notice if your students feel cared for and emotionally literate and, more importantly, so will the students themselves. Although, it's always about the students, not Ofsted criteria.

Good mental health support isn't an intervention; it's the foundation. Inclusion includes helping students understand themselves, relate to others and access learning without being overwhelmed by emotional dysregulation. A curriculum that cares for student's inner lives is smart, strategic and, in the long run, hugely effective in supporting their ability to learn (Durlak et al., 2011).

Building emotional literacy and regulation

If we want emotionally literate adults, we need to start with emotionally articulate children. If we want calm, self-aware learners, we need emotionally supportive environments. Emotional vocabulary and regulation strategies work hand in hand: students can't regulate what they can't name.

Labelling emotions helps shift children from reactive behaviour ('I'm lashing out') to reflective thinking ('I'm feeling overwhelmed'). Teaching this language explicitly from the early years gives all children a toolkit for navigating their own emotions and for understanding those of others. From nursery upwards, we should be teaching that 'sad' and 'angry' are just the tip of the iceberg. Words like 'frustrated', 'anxious', 'embarrassed', 'excluded' or 'hopeful' should become part of everyday classroom vocabulary.

Why regulation strategies matter

Children can't learn if their nervous system is in fight, flight, freeze or fawn. The student who has a meltdown in maths after break isn't 'choosing' bad behaviour – they're dysregulated. When you embed consistent approaches to regulation, you'll move from reacting to incidents to preventing them.

From the EYFS to Year 6 and beyond, regulation strategies should be part of daily school life. These are simple, effective routines that give students the language, tools and permission to manage how they're feeling.

Practical strategies to embed emotional literacy and regulation

- **Calm boxes or kits:** Have tactile, sensory resources in each classroom to support regulation.
- **Co-regulation scripts:** Short phrases to guide adults as they help children regulate, e.g. 'I wonder if you're in the yellow zone right now? What might help you move to green?'.
- **Emotion coaching:** A way of responding to behaviour by validating emotions and teaching problem-solving rather than escalating (Gottman et al., 1996).
- **Feelings check-ins:** Regular moments for children to reflect on and name how they are feeling. This can be as simple as a feelings board, visual cards or a colour-coded system.
- **Literacy links:** Books offer huge opportunities to explore the characters' emotional worlds. Go beyond plot: ask 'How do you think she felt when...?' and 'Why might he have acted that way?'
- **Modelling from adults:** Staff who appropriately name their feelings in context ('I'm feeling a bit stressed so I'm going to take a few deep breaths') provide powerful examples.
- **Regulation timetables:** Structured times for movement breaks, sensory activities or mindfulness, particularly for students with SEMH needs.
- **Supporting parents:** Share your regulation strategies and language with parents. They might even need support with their own regulation.
- **The 'Feelings Furballs':** Twelve characters aligned with the Zones of Regulation colours, designed to expand emotional vocabulary. Accessible across the primary age range and beyond.
- **Word walls and displays:** Make emotional language visible in every classroom. Feelings vocabulary wheels work well for this.
- **Zones of Regulation:** A colour-coded system to help children identify their emotional state and use regulation tools (Kuypers, 2011). Useful for establishing shared language across the school.

Embedding emotional literacy and regulation across your school

Embedding emotional literacy and regulation begins with staff training. Adults need to understand the approaches they are using and why they matter. Choose a framework that suits your setting, but adapt it rather than forcing a model that doesn't fit your students.

Daily modelling is essential. Every adult, in every classroom and space, including office staff, should use the same language and approaches. Make this language visible through displays, prompts and shared vocabulary so it becomes part of everyday school life.

Integrate emotional literacy and regulation into behaviour and restorative systems. Questions such as 'What zone were you in?' or 'What was your body telling you then?' help students connect their actions to their internal state.

Finally, build in regular review. Consider what's working, what needs adjusting and how staff and students are responding. As with so much in this book, embedding these approaches is an ongoing process, not a one-off initiative.

SEND considerations and beyond primary

Many pupils with SEND find emotional and sensory regulation particularly challenging, so that strong, whole-school approach offers consistency, scaffolding and a sense of safety. Students with autism often benefit from predictability and visual supports (see Chapter 8). Those with trauma or attachment difficulties may need co-regulation with a trusted adult before they are able to regulate independently. Pupils with ADHD may simply need regular opportunities for movement and sensory breaks built into the school day.

Support for emotional vocabulary and regulation shouldn't end at Year 6; in many ways, it becomes even more essential in secondary school. Hormonal changes, social pressures and high-stakes assessment can create a perfect storm for dysregulation. Students in Year 8 need the same core toolkit as those in Year 2, just adapted in an age-appropriate way. Older pupils often lack the language to articulate what is happening internally, making explicit teaching of emotional vocabulary just as important at Key Stage 3 as it is in the early years.

Your role as a leader: embedding SEMH support

- **Audit and embed:** Review where and how SEMH is currently taught and integrated across the curriculum. Ensure it's not dependent on PSHE or the SENDCo.
- **Celebrate success:** Highlight where this work is making a difference. Celebrate emotionally literate classrooms in the same way you celebrate academic success.
- **Fund the tools:** Training, resources and time all matter and need investment.
- **Lead by example:** Model vulnerability, openness and positive emotional communication. Use emotional vocabulary when speaking with staff and students.
- **Monitor impact:** Use student voice, behaviour data and staff feedback to track progress.
- **Prioritise CPD:** Give staff training on emotional literacy, trauma-informed practice, emotion coaching and de-escalation strategies.
- **Review behaviour policies:** Ensure they reflect inclusive values and offer regulated responses to emotional dysregulation, not just punishment.

Learning mentors: the power of trusted relationships

If we want students to thrive, they need relationships that extend beyond the classroom door. Learning mentors are one of the most underrated and most powerful parts of a school's inclusion toolkit. They're not simply 'extra adults'; they're trusted bridges between students, staff and families. With the right person in the role and enough dedicated time, the impact can be transformational.

Students learn best when they feel seen, safe and supported. Not every pupil receives that solely from their class teacher. Some need a consistent adult who is not marking their work, checking uniform or leading a lesson; someone who can hold them to account while offering unconditional support. That's where learning mentors come in. They're advocates, translators, emotional anchors and reality-checkers. They listen. They challenge. They show up every day (sometimes when others don't), and they do much of their work quietly: in corridors, at lunch, or on the edge of playground chaos.

What learning mentors actually do

Learning mentors build relationships with students who need an additional adult to champion them. They act as a consistent check-in point through daily chats, behaviour reviews and emotional coaching. They support self-regulation, goal setting, friendship difficulties and family worries; whatever is getting in the way of learning. They link home and school, helping parents navigate systems and ensuring students' voices are heard. They help teachers understand what lies beneath behaviour, because 'He's just lazy' is rarely the full story. They track progress, celebrate small wins and stay with students for the long game.

Embedding learning mentors effectively

Choosing the right people matters. Learning mentors need warmth, patience, humour and resilience. Experience with vulnerable students helps, but being deeply human matters just as much. Sometimes the right person arrives without the right experience; be prepared to train them.

- **Give them time.** Strong relationships are built slowly and consistently. Occasional conflict can even strengthen a relationship: trust grows when adults acknowledge their own mistakes.
- **Back them up.** If a mentor says a student needs something, listen.
- **Clarify the role.** They're not classroom cover or lunchtime supervisors. They are skilled support for complex needs. Protect their time and ensure they have clear line management.
- **Provide training** in the areas your cohort needs most — attachment, trauma, coaching, SLCN, SEND and working with parents.
- **Protect their capacity.** A mentor working meaningfully with 8–12 students is far more effective than one stretched across 40.

SEND considerations and secondary schools

Learning mentors are often the first adults to spot undiagnosed SEND because they see what happens in the unstructured spaces of school life. For students with additional needs, mentors provide essential support in navigating day-to-day challenges that may not be visible in the classroom. Students frequently disclose concerns to them too, adding an important safeguarding dimension, and mentors can help plan next steps safely and effectively.

Secondary schools may use pastoral leads or inclusion workers in similar roles, but the principle is the same: trusted relationships make everything else possible. Learning mentors at secondary can support attendance, transitions, post-16 decisions and emotional regulation at a time when students often need help most but are least likely to ask for it.

Your role

Value the role. Make it clear to staff and families that mentors are essential members of the school community, not a bolt-on luxury. Protect their time and their purpose so the work can actually have depth. Invest in their training and draw on their insights when planning provision; they see things others may miss. Involve them in SEND reviews, EHCP processes and reintegration plans so their knowledge shapes decisions, not merely responds to them.

Don't forget the people doing the holding. Provide supervision; this is emotionally demanding work, and mentors need space to reflect, decompress and recharge. Celebrate their success stories and share them widely. Track the impact of mentoring over time, even when the progress is messy or non-linear. This is the kind of work that transforms journeys quietly but powerfully, and it deserves to be recognised.

The SLCN-friendly school

We explored SLCN as a specific area of need in Chapter 8, so this section focuses on creating a whole-school environment where communication is prioritised. If a child can't understand what's being said, they can't follow instructions, access the curriculum, join discussions or make friends easily. Many students arrive at school with delayed or limited language, particularly those from disadvantaged backgrounds, and the gap just widens unless we act early and consistently.

SLCN is also commonly mislabelled as '(bad) behaviour', 'low ability' or simply 'quiet', whereas underneath there's frequently a language difficulty that needs unpicking. The good news is that you can do a lot without waiting for a diagnosis or referral.

What an SLCN-friendly school looks like

An SLCN-friendly school has classrooms rich in spoken and visual language: clear routines, visual timetables, symbols and dual coding. Adults check for understanding rather than compliance, using prompts such as 'Can you tell me what you need to do first?'

Targeted screening on entry, particularly in the EYFS and Key Stage 1, helps identify concerns early. Tools such as WellComm, Language Link or the Nuffield Early Language Intervention can support this process. Explicit vocabulary teaching across subjects, using tiered vocabulary systems, ensures language is taught systematically. Language scaffolds (e.g. sentence stems, word banks and writing frames) should be available to all children, not only those with an EHCP.

Classrooms should offer calm, low-pressure opportunities for talk, including some 'no hands up' time, think-pair-share and adults modelling sentences with warmth and patience. Short, focused language interventions, such as Talk Boost or WellComm follow-ups, can accelerate progress. Meaningful opportunities for talk and role-play across the curriculum allow students to use and embed new language.

Supporting students with SLCN

For those with identified SLCN, autism or learning difficulties, a consistent communication-friendly environment is essential. Some will need targeted SaLT. Where budgets allow, commissioning a speech therapist to assess, train staff or co-deliver interventions will have long-term impact, but where that isn't possible, upskilling staff in core strategies is the next best option and is cost-effective alongside standard NHS referrals.

Students who mask or appear shy are often overlooked but a pupil who isn't disrupting learning can still be struggling to understand. Some students, particularly girls, learn to just nod and smile rather than admit confusion. Silence is sometimes a red flag for unrecognised SLCN. Build space for every child to be heard through small-group work, pre-teaching or adult-led dialogue. Aim to create a supportive learning community where not understanding is okay.

SLCN support beyond primary

SLCN doesn't just disappear after Year 6; in fact, language demands increase in secondary just as adult support decreases. Students expected to access abstract texts, complex vocabulary and multiple teachers often struggle without scaffolds. Secondary schools need to build on primary strategies, particularly in subjects such as science, maths and history, where vocabulary becomes technical and nuanced. Screening the Year 7 intake is essential, as behaviour concerns can mask underlying and unmet language needs.

Your role in creating an SLCN-friendly school

Screening in the EYFS, Year 3 and Year 7 should be routine, forming the foundation of a whole-school approach to communication. Alongside this, staff training is essential — every teacher is a teacher of language — so invest in whole-school CPD on SLCN and inclusive communication. These principles should be embedded across policies, from curriculum planning to behaviour responses, and reflected in the environment through clear displays, symbols and vocabulary prompts in every classroom.

Where possible, work with specialists, but avoid relying solely on external support. Celebrate communication throughout school life, whether through assemblies, newsletters or parent workshops, so that language remains a visible, shared priority. Being SLCN-friendly requires intention, consistency and a belief that language belongs to everyone, not only those with a formal diagnosis.

Literacy difficulty-friendly schools

We explored dyslexia and literacy difficulties as a specific learning need in Chapter 8. Here, the focus shifts to creating classrooms and systems that actually work for how dyslexic learners learn, not just what we expect them to produce.

Dyslexia affects around ten per cent of the population (British Dyslexia Association, 2023), making it one of the most common specific learning difficulties. Yet many students still slip through the net. A dyslexia-friendly school doesn't just help those with a diagnosis. Good practice for dyslexia is simply good practice.

Dyslexia is widely misunderstood. The brain processes language, particularly reading, writing, spelling and working memory differently; it isn't a sign of low intelligence or ability. But the impact can be far-reaching: when a student is constantly having to work twice as hard to keep up, it chips away at organisation, confidence and behaviour. It's exhausting!

Many people with dyslexia spend years masking or muddling through. Some never receive a formal diagnosis or any significant extra support, especially in schools stretched thin by high levels of need. But they still need (and deserve) help. The right environment makes all the difference. My son is dyslexic. His spoken language and vocabulary are exceptionally strong, but his reading lagged years behind, leaving him really frustrated and demoralised. His experience is the reality for so many dyslexic children, who are bright, capable and trying far harder than anyone realises.

What does a dyslexia-friendly classroom look like?

A dyslexia-friendly classroom removes unnecessary barriers so students can focus their energy on learning, not on battling the environment around them:

- **assistive technology** – text-to-speech, speech-to-text and predictive spelling tools
- **clear, uncluttered displays** – visual noise can be overwhelming, so keep things purposeful and consistent
- **coloured exercise books** or paper where needed
- **dyslexia-friendly fonts and large, well-spaced text** – Comic Sans, Arial or Verdana are more accessible than decorative fonts
- **explicit teaching of metacognitive strategies** – modelling how to plan, organise and check work
- **extra time** for processing, planning and producing written work – slow processing is not slow thinking
- **feedback focused on content first**, then spelling and grammar in a manageable way
- **frequent low-stakes retrieval** to support memory and reduce overwhelm
- **high-frequency word walls** and spelling scaffolds that are visible and used daily
- **instructions chunked and repeated** – verbally, visually and written down where possible
- **opportunities to show learning in different ways** – oral answers, diagrams, voice notes or typing
- **pastel backgrounds or overlays** – bright whiteboards or paper can make text harder to track.

Supporting students with dyslexia

A dyslexia-friendly school doesn't wait for a diagnosis. Most support strategies are simply BPT (see Chapter 7), and many cost very little. However, if there's a persistent pattern of difficulty — particularly around phonological awareness, working memory or processing speed — screening can be useful. Tools such as GL's LASS and the Nessy screener offer a gentle first step, giving schools an early indication of potential literacy or processing difficulties long before a specialist assessment is on the table.

Dyslexia often co-occurs with other difficulties, including DCD (dyspraxia), ADHD or anxiety. Strengths-based conversations matter. Many dyslexic students are exceptional problem-solvers, storytellers or creative thinkers; they just need a system that plays to their strengths.

Clear communication with parents is vital. Be explicit about the difference between a school-based screener and a formal diagnosis. Many families assume schools can diagnose dyslexia or that an EP will automatically see their child. Be transparent about what is available in reality. Early access to technology also makes a huge difference: the sooner students use the tools that help them, the better.

Dyslexia support beyond primary

By secondary school, many undiagnosed dyslexic students have internalised years of feeling inadequate. They may avoid reading aloud, dodge homework or withdraw entirely. Supporting them means continuing to scaffold, not withdrawing support the moment they can decode text. Reading fluency, comprehension, spelling and written organisation still need attention — often alongside exam access arrangements and consistent use of assistive technology.

Your role in creating a dyslexia-friendly school

Start with your environment: how dyslexia-friendly are your classrooms, corridors and displays? Provide CPD so teachers genuinely understand what dyslexia is and how to adapt their practice. Screen early, but make it clear that screening is indicative, not diagnostic. Don't wait for students to fall significantly behind before investigating possible barriers.

Invest in practical resources: pastel paper, overlays, text-to-speech software and staff training all go a long way. Ensure dyslexia features in your teaching and learning strategy, not just your SEND report. Model a strengths-based ethos – celebrate the full range of achievement, not only what appears neatly written on the page. Children with dyslexic tendencies often excel in practical subjects and creative problem-solving. Bridge the primary–secondary gap by sharing access arrangements and strategies that work.

The outward-facing school

If we want families to be fully on board with education, we need to do more than open the school gates, we need to step outside them. Schools that work in partnership with their communities do more than improve outcomes for children; they build trust, resilience and social capital. They become anchors for families navigating increasingly complex challenges.

This approach is not just for early years or primary schools. Secondary schools can also act as hubs, particularly around post-16 options, mental health support and the realities of teenage life.

When children arrive at school hungry, tired, dysregulated or unsupported, their ability to learn is immediately compromised. Instead of leaning on familiar narratives about what families 'should' be doing, outward-facing schools ask, 'What can we do to help make that possible?'

This doesn't mean taking on every social issue or replacing other services. It means rethinking what it means to serve a community and recognising that investment in families pays off in engagement, attendance (see Chapter 13) and achievement. Families most in need of support are often those with children experiencing SEND or SEMH needs, and their parents/carers may have unmet needs of their own.

What might an outward-facing school look like?

An outward-facing school builds genuine partnership with families and the wider community, meeting needs with practicality and respect. Ideas include:

- **Parent drop-ins and support groups** – not only for SEND or behaviour, but budgeting, literacy, CV writing, sleep routines or screen time, depending on what families need.
- **Food banks or partnerships with local charities** – some schools run on-site food banks to reduce stigma and improve access.

- **Workshops and family learning** – support for parents on everything from phonics to parenting; the more confident parents feel, the more able they are to help at home.
- **Early Years and toddler groups** – some trusts build strong foundations by supporting families even before children reach Reception.
- **Community outreach** – going beyond the school newsletter with local events, pop-up support in community centres and coffee mornings to help bridge gaps.
- **Home visits** that aren't just about attendance – relational, respectful conversations at home can transform trust and give staff insight into a family's everyday challenges.

Supporting SEND families

Parents of children with SEND often feel isolated or unheard. Creating informal, non-judgemental spaces where families can share experiences and get advice from staff and from each other can transform your relationship with them. Consider setting up a parent group facilitated by a member of SLT or the SENDCo (see Part 3 for more on supporting SENDCos).

Your role in building community partnerships

Look at what's already working. Do your families trust you? Where are the gaps? Engage with local services and find out what's already available, maybe you could co-deliver something or strengthen an existing partnership? Create time for this work; time, training and funding will be needed if your community engagement is to be sustainable. Involve your families; ask what they need, and listen. Model empathy: community engagement should be relational, not transactional.

Celebrate your community by showcasing successes, valuing every parent voice and bringing families into school in meaningful, purposeful ways. Supporting the community and student SEMH, SLCN and literacy needs across your school is about building systems that hold and relationships that matter.

13 Improving attendance

You can't teach a child who isn't in the room. We all know this. But improving attendance isn't about sending more letters home or pulling families through formal processes. You need to understand what sits behind the absences and build a school where children want to be. Attendance goes hand in hand with supporting your local community (Chapter 12). A student who misses a day a week loses 39 days of education a year (DfE, 2024); that's almost an entire half-term gone. It's more than academic loss: attendance is tied to friendships, routines, wellbeing and safeguarding.

Most parents aren't trying to be difficult. They're also potentially managing work, housing insecurity, transport, SEND, mental health, other dependants... the list goes on. Shaming or chasing usually has the opposite effect. Instead, you need to build trust, offer support and remove barriers. Sometimes a student's education is simply not very high on a family's agenda, but you can gently help raise the status and importance of schooling.

Attendance drops sharply in secondary (DfE, 2024). Teenagers may be disengaged, anxious or navigating complicated family dynamics. They need the same warmth and consistency we offer in the EYFS, just in a more age-appropriate way (form-tutor check-ins, breakfast clubs, quiet spaces or mentoring).

What works in improving attendance?

Improving attendance works best when we focus on simple, human approaches that build trust rather than pressure. Here are some ideas:

- **First-day response** – a quick call to check in with absent families. Not accusatory, just a 'We missed them today. Is everything OK?' to show you care, not surveillance.
- **Mentor or key-adult support** – regular contact with a trusted adult makes all the difference, especially for persistently absent students.
- **Attendance clinics** – not a telling-off, but a conversation: what's getting in the way, and how can we help?
- **Home visits** – sometimes a friendly knock at the door does more than ten attendance letters.

- **Celebrating small wins** – for some, even one day of attendance is an achievement, so praise progress, not perfection.
- **Links to mental health support** – anxiety or stress often sit behind poor attendance; link families with CAMHS, ELSAs or counselling where you can.
- **Make school a place they want to be** – think nurture, relationships and belonging; if students feel safe and connected, they're far more likely to turn up.
- **Staff training** – make it clear to staff that late arrivals should be welcomed warmly; a genuine 'nice to see you' goes much further than a 'sit down, you're late'.

School avoidance

We talk a lot about attendance data, but behind every persistent absence is a person who is often anxious, overwhelmed and unable to cope with school in its current form. School avoidance is a signal. If we ignore it, students become more distant, the gap grows and returning gets harder. This is also why the terminology has shifted away from 'school refusal': these pupils aren't refusing; they *can't*.

What is school avoidance?

Sometimes called emotionally based school avoidance (EBSA), this is when a pupil experiences significant anxiety about attending school. It's often rooted in fear: maybe fear of failure, or separation, sensory overload, social pressure or past trauma. It's increasing, and, in primary especially, when a student shows early signals it is important to act before the issues escalate. Prevention is cheaper, emotionally and financially, than supporting students back into school further down the line.

Early warning signs

- Frequent unexplained absences or lateness.
- Requests to go home due to vague illness.
- A student who seems fine in class but is melting down at home.
- Repeated visits to the medical room.
- Avoidance of particular subjects, spaces or staff.

What works for school avoiders

The longer a student is away, the harder it is to return: each missed day reinforces the fear. This is why the answer is rarely a stern attendance letter, but a tailored, compassionate reintegration plan. There is no single fix, but a multi-pronged, relationship-based approach helps. Start by identifying the root cause: attendance and pastoral teams need to work together, drawing on student voice, parental insight and staff observation. Common causes include:

- anxiety (often undiagnosed)
- sensory sensitivities
- bullying or friendship issues
- unmet SEND
- attachment difficulties
- academic overwhelm.

Families aren't always part of the problem, they're often the ones holding the emotional fallout. Build relationships based on trust rather than blame. Invite them in early, listen without judgement and co-design a plan together.

Returning after absence shouldn't feel like a punishment. Avoid making a big fuss, putting the student on the spot or overwhelming them with catch-up work. Small but impactful strategies include:

- a meet-and-greet from a key adult on arrival
- an adjusted timetable, even just for mornings or certain subjects
- access to a safe space or calm room
- one consistent adult to check in with regularly
- a home–school journal to bridge the gap
- briefing peers and staff so the student is welcomed back without a fuss.

Some pupils will also need input from CAMHS, an Emotional Literacy Support Assistant (ELSA) or an educational psychologist, and some families may benefit from parenting support or early help. Keep an updated directory of local provision and be ready to refer. If you're not making progress, keep escalating.

For students who aren't in school

Virtual contact can be a lifeline. A teacher recording a brief 'hello' message, an invitation to watch a school assembly online, or a pastoral call that isn't about guilt or attendance data keeps the relationship alive and the door open.

Where appropriate, also consider:

- a phased return plan, with very small steps agreed with the student
- dual registration with an AP or hospital school
- outreach support from a mentor or trusted adult
- reintegration meetings focused on strengths and next steps, not blame.

SEND and inclusion considerations

Persistent absence can be a significant indicator of unmet SEND needs, especially autism, SLCN or attachment difficulties. Is the environment overwhelming? Are transitions too tricky? Is masking exhaustion taking its toll? Early identification and support are key. Work closely with parents and listen to the student. It's also worth auditing whether your provision is genuinely inclusive. If your environment is overly rigid, noisy or high-pressure, it may be contributing to avoidance in the first place. Do your systems build safety and belonging, or do they just chase compliance?

SLT responsibilities

Improving attendance isn't just a classroom task. It depends on a culture shaped from the top. *You* play a vital role in creating the conditions where children feel safe, supported and able to attend.

- Your attendance policy should reflect a relationship-first approach, balancing expectations with empathy and allowing for compassionate flexibility, especially where mental health or SEND are involved.
- Train staff to view attendance as a wellbeing issue, not just a data one – and include EBSA awareness in CPD so that teachers know what to look for and what to do.
- Make attendance everyone's responsibility, not just the office manager's or the Educational Welfare Officer's.

- Create a clear bridge between your attendance lead, SENDCo, pastoral lead and class teachers.
- Use data wisely: look for patterns, not percentages. Who's slipping through the cracks?
- Celebrate improvements, not only 100 per cent attendance. A student moving from 65 per cent to 85 per cent deserves just as much recognition.
- Link attendance with wider inclusion work and triangulate with safeguarding and pastoral support.
- Ensure your SENDCo is engaged with data linking SEND and attendance.
- For school avoiders, apply for an EHCNA even if the student isn't currently in school, because it will take significant support to re-engage them.
- Advocate. If external agencies aren't moving quickly enough, push for EHCPs, ELSA referrals or Tier 2 mental health input.

Improving attendance has moved a long way in recent years, and best practice has gone from nagging to nurturing. When we treat school avoidance as a message rather than misbehaviour, and show children and families that they belong, their presence matters and that help is available, attendance can be improved naturally and sustainably.

14 Nurture provision

'Nurture' is one of those buzzwords that has been around schools for a while. It sounds lovely: warm, cosy, a bit like a hug in educational form. But what actually *is* nurture provision? How can schools get it right? On my travels around settings I've seen the full spectrum, from amazing to ineffective to actively detrimental to pupil development. The worst example I encountered involved staff with limited training working with pupils whose needs were incompatible, and the trust lead thought it was the best thing ever. *That* was a fun conversation...

What is nurture provision?

At its heart, nurture provision is a structured approach to supporting children whose emotional, social or behavioural needs are getting in the way of their learning. It's based on the original work of Marjorie Boxall (you may have heard of a Boxall Profile) in the 1960s and 70s, which found that some children struggle in school not because they lack ability, but because their early experiences – often traumatic or disrupted – mean they need a different kind of support.

A good nurture group or nurture approach creates a small, safe, consistent space where children feel valued and understood. It focuses on developing:

- social skills
- emotional regulation
- confidence and self-esteem
- positive relationships with adults and peers.

The idea is to repair and build those foundational 'soft skills' so children can better access mainstream learning.

When is nurture appropriate?

Nurture provision is not a catch-all. It is not the answer for every child with behaviour that challenges, nor is it a replacement for specialist SEND support, specialist school places where required, or mental health interventions.

It *is* appropriate when children:

- show social, emotional or behavioural difficulties that interfere with their learning
- have experienced early trauma, attachment difficulties, or disrupted home lives
- struggle with peer relationships or regulating emotions in the classroom
- need a lower-stimulus environment to feel safe and ready to learn.

It is especially useful for children in the early years or KS1/KS2 who have not yet developed the coping strategies to manage in a large classroom. Increasingly, KS3 and KS4 schools are also operating hubs where learning can be more flexible.

How to do nurture well

Getting nurture right takes more than a comfortable room and some colouring pencils. It requires:

- **A focus on relationship-building, not just behaviour management:** it's easy to slip into 'controlling behaviour' mode, but nurture is about supporting emotional growth first. The aim is always to support pupils in getting back to class more often, so a hybrid model is useful.
- **A trained practitioner:** nurture work isn't something you simply slot into the timetable. Staff need specialist training to understand the theory behind nurture, attachment and how to build relationships that support change. The Nurture UK programme and Boxall training are well-regarded options. You can get provision up and running without training if you already have the right staff in place, as long as there's ongoing CPD.
- **Clear communication and planning:** the nurture group must connect with the child's class teachers, SENDCo and parents or carers. Progress and strategies should be shared and consistent.
- **Consistent, predictable routines:** students thrive on knowing what to expect. Nurture groups need a clear timetable with familiar activities, though flexibility matters too.

- **Small group sizes:** ideally six to eight children maximum, to ensure staff can build genuine, responsive relationships.
- **Whole-school buy-in:** nurture is not an isolated intervention. It should be part of a broader culture of emotional support and understanding across the school. Teachers and support staff outside the nurture group need to understand each student's needs and strategies. Those working in the provision need to feel part of the school community, and children should have a base class as well. Their base-class teacher should ideally have some input into planning and assessment, especially where there is no qualified teacher in the provision (though a highly skilled HLTA can also work well with the right person in post).

What happens when nurture isn't done well?

Nurture provision done badly can do more harm than good, turning what should be a safe space into just another stressful environment for pupils. Common pitfalls include:

- **Focusing only on behaviour management:** when the emotional and relational work is skipped, nurture becomes a behavioural detention with an inclusive-sounding name – ineffective and demoralising for all.
- **Inconsistent staffing or routines:** frequent changes in staff or unpredictable schedules make attendees anxious and undo any progress.
- **Isolation from the rest of school:** if nurture groups are 'hidden away' and communication is poor, pupils may feel singled out or struggle to reintegrate.
- **Lack of training or understanding:** when staff don't understand nurture theory, the group can become a 'time out' space rather than a supportive environment. This risks stigmatising students rather than helping them.
- **Overloading the group:** trying to serve too many students dilutes the individual attention each one needs.

The consequences? Increased anxiety for children, no real progress in emotional regulation, and sometimes a worsening of behaviour because the root causes aren't being addressed.

Considerations for SLT

Setting up and maintaining effective nurture provision is a direction many schools are now exploring to support growing need. For school leaders, there are some important strategic and operational factors to bear in mind.

- **Be realistic about capacity:** avoid overloading nurture groups. Know your limits and do not dilute quality by trying to serve too many children. Sometimes alternative or additional provision is needed.
- **Communication:** embed strong communication channels between nurture staff, class teachers, the SENDCo and parents or carers. This collaboration ensures strategies are consistent and children do not feel 'split' between environments.
- **Data and impact:** collect meaningful data on children's social and emotional progress alongside academic outcomes. Share successes and areas for development with governors and senior leaders to demonstrate impact.
- **Investment in training:** ensure your nurture staff have access to recognised training. This cannot be overlooked or skimped on.
- **Parent and community engagement:** actively involve parents in the nurture process. Many children's emotional difficulties relate to home circumstances, so family engagement can be critical to success.
- **Plan set-up carefully:** take time to get things right from the start and ensure the provision is well resourced. Go and see other nurture settings in action before you begin.
- **Safeguarding and wellbeing:** recognise that children in nurture provision may be particularly vulnerable. Ensure robust safeguarding procedures are in place and that nurture practitioners are vigilant and well supported. Adults working in this area also need additional support, and a clinical supervision model is worth considering.
- **Staffing and resources:** provide protected time and space for nurture practitioners to do their work effectively. Avoid rotating staff in and out, as consistency is crucial.
- **Transitions and inclusion:** plan carefully for children moving back into mainstream classes or to other provision. Nurture should prepare children for reintegration, not create an unintended permanent 'bubble'. Even where

a pupil is waiting for a specialist placement, include them in whole-school and classroom life as much as possible.

- **Vision and ethos:** embed nurture as part of your whole-school approach to wellbeing and inclusion. Nurture shouldn't be a bolt-on or a last resort but a respected and integral part of your offer.

Enhanced provision: what it means and how to become one

Some schools choose to develop their nurture groups into an enhanced provision, which is a more formalised, resourced and recognised specialist intervention for pupils with specific needs such as SEMH or SLCN. There are many overlaps with nurture, but these provisions are generally developed in conjunction with the local authority and have funding attached.

Key features of enhanced nurture provision include:

- **Clear inclusion pathways:** enhanced provisions often form part of a graduated response, supporting children to transition successfully back to mainstream provision or to specialist placements where appropriate.
- **Dedicated specialist staff:** often including practitioners with higher-level SEND qualifications or therapeutic skills.
- **Formal partnerships:** working closely with local authorities, educational psychologists and external agencies to secure funding, advice and multi-agency support.
- **More comprehensive assessment and planning:** including detailed baseline assessments, individual targets and personalised support plans aligned with EHCPs where applicable.
- **Robust quality assurance:** regular external review and accreditation (for example, through Nurture UK's Enhanced Provision recognition) to ensure standards are met and provision improves continually.
- **Smaller group sizes and higher staff ratios:** to meet more intensive needs effectively.
- **Therapeutic approaches:** some enhanced provisions integrate counselling, play therapy or mental health interventions alongside nurture work.

Becoming an enhanced provision setting requires strong leadership, investment in staff development, clear evidence of impact and close collaboration with families and professionals. However, for schools with the capacity and desire to meet more complex SEMH needs in-house, it can be a transformative step.

Closing thoughts

Nurture provision is a powerful tool when done well. It is an intentional, trained approach that builds the relationships and emotional skills that are foundational to learning. When it works, students find a safe place to heal and grow; when it does not, it risks becoming just another label and a missed opportunity. The best nurture groups don't exist in isolation – they're part of an emotionally intelligent whole-school culture where every student is seen, supported and celebrated.

15 Systems, processes and assistive technology

Assistive technology and inclusive tech use

EdTech has exploded over the past decade, but not all tech is created equal. For pupils with SEND, technology can be a game-changer when it's used intentionally, not just because it's shiny and new. Sometimes, assistive technology doesn't just remove barriers, it opens doors. However, on the ground, staff can be worried about technology and not see the potential.

Why it matters

For some students, assistive technology can mean the difference between dependence and independence. Screen readers, speech-to-text tools, electronic spellcheckers and visual timetables all allow pupils to access the curriculum in ways that are matched to their needs, not our assumptions.

Tech isn't a cure-all, of course. It needs to be introduced with care, embedded into classroom practice and supported by staff who understand both the tools and the students using them. Tech that's gathering dust in a cupboard isn't assistive, it's expensive and pointless.

What it should look like

Start with an audit. What tech is already in place? What's being used regularly and effectively? What sits unused because staff didn't get training, or because no one ever checked whether it met the needs of the pupil it was bought for? Next, look at digital inclusion as a whole-school issue. Are your online platforms, learning portals or resources accessible? Can pupils with visual impairments, literacy difficulties or processing differences navigate them? Is the tech available for everyone who needs it or is it rationed because of budget or bandwidth?

Pupils with dyslexia or tracking difficulties may benefit from reading pens or coloured overlays. Those with ADHD or executive functioning difficulties may need visual timers, voice reminders or structured apps to support organisation.

Speech-to-text software can support children with writing difficulties, and the mighty iPad is often the most versatile tool when the apps are chosen carefully.

Assistive tech also supports staff. It reduces workload when used well (e.g. automated reader tools for assessment access arrangements) and makes feedback more accessible through audio and video options.

Starting early is also key. Ensuring that students with the highest needs access as much as they can early on is so important so they can be familiar with software and accessibility and use it to their advantage ready for Year 6 SATs and beyond (but hopefully if you're reading this a few years post-publication, SATs will have been scrapped already!).

Making tech the norm is highly inclusive. Having text-reading pens available for a variety of pupils to use is a good start. They aren't cheap but are evidence-based. As students get older, they can be really averse to appearing different from their peers and having tech available for more pupils is a way to combat this. Also consider that teaching pupils to be self-sufficient on a laptop can reduce the number of LSA hours they need overall due to increased independence. It's win-win.

Your responsibilities

- Audit current use of assistive technology across year groups and key stages – what's working, what's missing and what needs training.
- Invest in devices and software that directly match identified pupil needs.
- Provide regular CPD on assistive technology use – include SENDCos, IT leads and class teachers in the training.
- Embed inclusive design into digital platforms, ensuring accessibility features are standard practice, not add-ons.
- Establish processes for evaluating the impact of tech on pupil progress and engagement.
- Build inclusive tech use into wider teaching and learning strategies – not just for pupils with EHCPs.
- Plan for sustainability – budget for updates, repairs, replacements and ongoing licences.

Assistive tech isn't about giving some students an unfair advantage. It's about giving all children what they need to succeed. Often, the tools that support our most vulnerable learners end up benefiting everyone.

Staff CPD and induction focused on SEND

SEND provision is a thread running through everything: planning, behaviour, wellbeing and curriculum delivery. So, SEND training can't be a bolt-on. It has to be stitched into the fabric of school life, starting at staff induction and growing through ongoing, relevant CPD.

Why it matters

Staff can't adapt to needs they don't understand. Even the most compassionate, committed teacher can make well-intentioned mistakes if they've never had training in the needs they're trying to support. Even teachers who are trained may not be confident. One child masking their anxiety might be mistaken for being 'fine', while another whose dyslexia makes reading out loud a horrible experience may be seen as disengaged.

We need to give every adult the tools to do their job with clarity and confidence.

Staff induction

For new staff, SEND induction is often their first encounter with your school's values around inclusion. That means going beyond just handing over the one-page profile pile. A robust induction can explain how to access key information, offer a clear explanation of how your school approaches good or better teaching and give practical examples of what inclusive practice looks like in your context. New staff can also be introduced to the wider team around the child, whether that's learning mentors, the SENDCo or pastoral leads, so they can put faces to job roles easily.

Embedding CPD throughout the year

SEND-focused CPD is most effective when it's built into the school year. That might be through spotlight sessions on neurodiversity, trauma-informed strategies or adaptive teaching. It might be linked to pupil case studies, lesson study or team teaching. What matters most is that it's ongoing and seen as core business, not a one-off.

Focus first on the most common areas of need – speech and language, autism, ADHD, SEMH and literacy-based difficulties. You don't need every staff member to become a SEND specialist, but they do need to understand how these needs present and what classroom adaptations are reasonable and effective. This is particularly important for early career teachers and support staff, who often find themselves managing pupils with high needs with little prior experience. Also consider any agency staff who are supporting, as they can turn up woefully unprepared.

Whole-school wellbeing

Staff wellbeing is the bedrock of any school aiming for long-term success in inclusive practice. When staff feel valued, supported and emotionally safe, they're more likely to stay, to innovate and to give their best to the pupils who need them most. Inclusion is a culture and that culture is shaped every day by the people delivering it.

High staff turnover can disrupt continuity for pupils with SEND and SEMH needs, many of whom rely on trusted relationships and predictable support. Prioritising wellbeing is about workload, respect, open communication and professional trust. If you want to attract and retain staff who are committed to excellent provision for all pupils, you have to build a working environment where they can thrive and develop. When they move on, it's because you've developed them for a promotion, not because the role was too stressful.

The speed of change

We're all in a rush. Especially as a leader, when we see the vastness of the task in front of us. Turning a giant cruise ship needs to be a slower process than if you just had a little fishing boat! I need some new analogies as I'm forever saying Rome wasn't built in a day... We forget that when we can so clearly see the bigger picture and have that clear vision of educational utopia, we don't want to drag our colleagues kicking and screaming. We want whole-school buy-in.

This means introducing change with care, compassion and realism. People don't resist change because they're obstructive; often, it's because they're overwhelmed, overworked or haven't yet seen how the change will support them or their students. Rushing in with several new initiatives at once rarely ends well (no matter how well-intentioned). I've found this out the hard way as I've been known to be somewhat over-enthusiastic, resulting in a lot of eyerolling from my staff!

If we want long-lasting, inclusive practice, we need to build trust and capacity first. Support staff through change by breaking it into manageable steps, offering regular feedback opportunities and celebrating small wins along the way. A culture of reflection and shared ownership is far more powerful than a checklist of mandates.

In the end, although school leaders create the educational climate of the school, meaningful change is rarely top-down – it's grown together, through time, relationships and a shared belief that we're heading somewhere better.

Appraisals

Embedding inclusive practice into your person-centred appraisal cycle sends a powerful message. It signals that inclusive teaching is excellent teaching. Staff targets can include adaptive practice, observations can explore how SEND pupils are being supported and professional development reviews can reflect on both individual and whole-school progress. This approach also encourages staff to view inclusion as part of their professional growth.

Your responsibilities

- Ensure every staff induction includes meaningful SEND content, tailored to the role.
- Plan CPD that revisits SEND regularly throughout the year.
- Use internal expertise and external partnerships to diversify training input.
- Map CPD provision with your SENDCo against the needs on your SEND register; where are the gaps in staff confidence or skill?
- Make inclusive practice a visible part of the appraisal process.
- Invest in time for staff to observe, coach and collaborate around inclusive teaching.
- Make sure your CPD is actually accessible; can support staff attend, and is the format inclusive?

When staff feel confident in supporting diverse needs, you get fewer escalations, better pupil outcomes and more resilient, reflective classrooms. Most importantly, you remove the potential lottery for pupils with SEND because their success doesn't depend on whether they happened to find a teacher who 'gets it'.

A whole-school transitions strategy

Transitions can be one of the most overlooked stress points in a child's school journey yet they're some of the most predictable. Every September, we ask pupils to walk into new rooms, face new routines and meet new adults, often with very little scaffolding to help them cope with that change. For many students, especially those with SEND, SEMH needs or anxiety, this isn't just unsettling; it can be genuinely destabilising. There are also day-to-day transitions which can be stressful.

Why transitions matter

Put simply, new expectations. For pupils with additional needs, this change can trigger spikes in anxiety, dips in behaviour or even school avoidance. It's not just about September. Mid-year moves, managed transitions, moving from KS1 to KS2 (or Year 6 to Year 7) all require thoughtful, joined-up planning to avoid worry.

When transitions are well-supported, you're not just managing logistics, you're building trust. Pupils feel safer, parents feel more confident and staff are better prepared to meet their class where they're at from day one.

What it could look like

A strong transitions strategy doesn't start in the final week of July, it's embedded throughout the year. For pupils with additional needs, this might include enhanced transition planning meetings, pupil passports shared well in advance or familiarisation visits to new settings and staff. Photos of new classrooms, visual timetables or even short video tours all help reduce the unknown.

Think about building in opportunities for relational handover, not just paperwork handover. A conversation between current and next teachers, a shared activity with the new class or even a meet-the-adult breakfast or playground walkabout can do more than a list of strategies ever will.

For pupils joining your school mid-year – or moving to a specialist setting – clear communication, staggered starts and parental partnership are key. The student should never be the last to know what's happening.

Secondary transitions deserve particular care. A single taster day in July won't cut it for vulnerable pupils. Start conversations early, offer multiple visits and build key relationships in advance. Also, don't forget to gather feedback: ask pupils what helped and what didn't.

Transitions from EYFS to Year 1

The move from Reception to Year 1 is one of the most significant and often underestimated transitions in a child's school journey, especially for pupils with additional needs. Developmentally, many children are simply not ready to leap from a play-based, exploratory curriculum to a formal, desk-based model overnight.

A more developmentally appropriate approach is to bridge the two phases, extending the principles of the EYFS curriculum into the autumn term of Year 1 and beyond where needed. Maintaining elements such as continuous provision, movement breaks, hands-on learning and emotional check-ins helps to preserve a sense of agency and wellbeing.

Transitions from Year 2 to Year 3

Equally important is the transition from Year 2 to Year 3, especially when this involves moving from an infant to a junior or primary school. Pupils who've grown used to a nurturing, familiar environment with consistent adults can find the jump to a more 'formal' KS2 setting disorientating, especially with additional needs thrown into the mix.

A supported transition strategy – including cross-phase visits, key adult introductions and gradual shifts in routine – can make a world of difference in helping pupils feel secure, valued and ready for what's next.

Your responsibilities

- Develop a whole-school transitions strategy that includes specific planning for vulnerable pupils.
- Ensure enhanced transition support is available for those with SEND, SEMH or who are identified as at risk.
- Allocate time for relational handovers between staff – not just data.
- Work with feeder and destination schools to build in joint working and early information sharing.
- Offer parents clear communication and opportunities to meet new staff.

- Monitor transition points for spikes in behaviour, anxiety or attendance – and intervene early.
- Celebrate positive transitions – share what worked to inform future planning. Consider key year groups especially.

Transitions can either be stumbling blocks or stepping stones. A robust strategy doesn't just reduce risk, it actively supports inclusion, belonging and emotional safety. No student should feel like they're starting from scratch just because they're moving rooms.

16 Formal processes: paperwork, assessment and accountability

The systems that document, track and report on SEND provision aren't just bureaucracy. When done well, they protect student's entitlements, support staff and demonstrate impact. When done poorly, they create so much workload without any clear purpose.

SEND paperwork: who goes on the register?

Deciding who goes on the SEND register should be a careful, evidence-led process, but in practice, this area remains plagued by inconsistency across schools and LAs. In some settings, the SEND register balloons to over 30 per cent of the cohort, while in others, pupils with clear needs are somehow missed entirely.

The data backs this up. A 2021 study by the Education Policy Institute (EPI) found enormous variation in the proportion of children identified with SEND. The research found that children with similar characteristics were more likely to be identified as having SEND in some schools than others, particularly in academies and schools with high accountability pressures. This variability raises fundamental questions: what does it actually mean to have SEND in one school versus another? Who decides, and based on what evidence?

The SEND register

The SEND register is a school-held list of children identified as requiring SEN support or an EHCP. Being on the register isn't about having a label, nor should it depend purely on a diagnosis. What it should reflect is a student's ongoing need for additional and different provision beyond what is ordinarily available in the classroom.

According to the SEND Code of Practice (2015, 6.36), a pupil is identified as having SEND if they have a learning difficulty or disability that requires special educational provision, namely provision that is 'additional to or different from' that made generally for others of the same age in a mainstream setting.

Diagnosis ≠ automatic inclusion

A diagnosis can help inform support, but it doesn't automatically mean a child needs to go on the SEND register.

Take, for instance, a pupil with diagnosed dyslexia who's progressing well due to best-quality teaching, scaffolded tasks and access to tools like coloured overlays or text-to-speech software. In this case, their needs are being fully met through universal provision. If they don't require additional or different provision to their peers (i.e. Tier Two or Tier Three support), they don't necessarily meet the criteria for SEN support.

This distinction matters. SENDCos therefore must use professional judgement and the graduated approach – assess, plan, do, review – as a rigorous decision-making tool. Blanket policies (e.g. 'everyone with ADHD is on the register' or 'you need an EHCP to be classed as SEND') aren't just unhelpful, they're unlawful. In cases where pupils do have a diagnosis but don't require anything over and above good classroom teaching, it may still be useful to have a one-page profile and for them to be on a watch or concern list.

Who is on your SEND register shouldn't ideally just be the SENDCo's decision. A discussion with senior leaders is key for joined-up thinking about who needs extra support. If your list is ballooning due to significant needs, then, unfortunately, so be it. All students who meet the criteria should be included.

The concern list

Some students sit in a grey area where there's *something*, but not yet something diagnosable or clearly defined. Perhaps they're struggling with expressive language, have intermittent sensory sensitivities or aren't quite catching up, despite interventions. This is where your concern or watch list becomes invaluable.

It may be useful to have a school-wide, formalised system (often RAG-rated[2] or flagged on the Management Information System) where staff can register pupils they're concerned about. This isn't the same as putting them on the SEND register; it's a pre-SEND flag designed to build a year-on-year picture.

[2] RAG-rated: a pupil is tagged Red, Amber or Green depending on the level of concern. Red – significant concern / needs urgent attention; amber – some concern / monitor closely; green – low concern / no immediate action. This gives a quick visual indicator of risk or need.

Concern/watch list: whole-school tool

1. All staff can raise concerns using a concern sheet (a template is downloadable from this book's companion website).
2. The SENDCo triages these and logs them centrally and observes pupils.
3. Class teachers implement a first wave of strategies from the QFT strategies toolkit or similar (also downloadable).
4. Concerns are reviewed termly through pupil progress and inclusion meetings.

The watch list serves several purposes. It helps track patterns over time: are the same pupils being referred repeatedly? It enables early intervention without over-pathologising what might be normal variation in development. It reassures parents that school is taking their child's needs seriously, even where the threshold for the SEND register hasn't yet been met.

This process also embeds a whole-school responsibility for SEND. It signals that not all students with additional needs need an 'official' SEND label from the outset. Sometimes what they need is BPT, minor adjustments, pastoral support and a watchful eye.

So, who should be on the register? Use the following guiding questions:

1. Is the student receiving provision that is additional to or different from that made for most other pupils?
2. Are they receiving regular adult-led intervention outside of usual classroom teaching?
3. Has a specialist (e.g. EP, SaLT) made formal recommendations for provision beyond quality-first teaching?
4. Is the provision specified and documented in an EHCP?
5. Is the pupil's progress significantly below age-related expectations *despite* high-quality universal teaching and differentiated provision?

If the answer is no to all of these, but concerns persist, or the pupil has a diagnosis but no additional needs over and above good teaching, use the concern list and flag them for monitoring. It may be that they'd benefit from a referral for ADHD/autism or another need.

Top Tip

If a parent asks for a referral for something like ADHD and you don't see any evidence for the need in class, support the parent anyway and refer. Firstly, it shows the parent that, as a school, you're supporting their concerns (tell them that there's not much evidence you can add from the school's perspective if the pupil doesn't have additional classroom needs) and secondly, we're not clinicians; it's not up to us to be the gatekeeper to a diagnosis. Yes, it's extra paperwork, but it's not for you to decide. If pupils come back with a diagnosis that school doesn't see in day-to-day practice, again, roll with it. You don't need to put them on the SEND list if their in school needs are low.

Required paperwork

When adding a student to the SEND register, it's important to distinguish between what's legally required under the SEND Code of Practice and relevant legislation, and what just constitutes best practice.

Legally required paperwork for SEN support

Under Section 6 of the SEND Code of Practice (2015) and the Children and Families Act 2014, schools must:

- identify and assess pupils with SEND using a graduated approach - assess, plan, do, review (6.44)
- keep a record of the provision being made for pupils with SEND (6.67)
- inform parents when special educational provision is being made (6.43)
- ensure that teaching is adapted to respond to the strengths and needs of all pupils (6.15–6.16)
- ensure the SEN information report on the school's website is up to date and reflects school practice (6.79).

This means that the minimum legal paperwork *must* include:

- a record of the child's SEN needs, including the nature of the learning difficulty or disability
- a record of SEN provision being made, demonstrating that it's additional to or different from what's available to all pupils
- evidence of parent/carer communication, including notification of SEN support status

- termly reviews of the support and progress being made (this may take the form of meeting notes, updated support plans or review summaries).

Note that there's no legal requirement for a specific document type (e.g. 'IEP', 'one-page profile'). The law requires that provision and progress are recorded and reviewed but how you do this is up to your setting.

Best practice paperwork

To ensure robust provision, accurate monitoring and preparedness for potential EHCP requests, many schools go beyond the legal minimum. Documents that are highly recommended but not statutory requirements include:

- **One-page profile**: captures pupil voice, strengths, challenges and helpful strategies. Promotes inclusion and ownership, especially useful for transitions or new staff.
- **Support plan/SEN support plan/IEP**: outlines specific outcomes, provision and strategies. Reviewed termly as part of the APDR cycle.
- **Whole-school provision map**: tracks group interventions, additional support and specialist input across the school. Helpful for SENDCos and governors to monitor cost-effectiveness and impact.
- **Evidence of assess, plan, do, review cycle**: documents how needs were assessed, what was planned, what was done and what progress was made. Forms the foundation of evidence for any future EHCP application or graduated response escalation.
- **Concern sheet**: used by staff to flag pupils not yet on the register but causing concern. Provides early evidence of emerging needs and intervention attempts.
- **Strategy toolkit**: offers tried-and-tested strategies for initial classroom support before escalation. Builds staff confidence and ensures consistent universal provision.
- **Meeting notes/parental communications log/intervention records**: keeps a clear record of conversations with parents or carers. Essential for transparency and safeguarding.

While not all of this is required by law, it is best practice to have a coherent, joined-up approach that shows clear identification, appropriate provision and measurable progress. Crucially, this paperwork should be live, succinct and useful.

Top Tip

Some helpful templates are available on this book's companion website.

Who goes on the SEND register is a nuanced, professional decision. A diagnosis may inform that decision, but it should never drive it. Your SEND register must reflect need. Use your concern list to monitor emerging issues, apply the graduated response diligently and never underestimate the power of excellent teaching and adaptation to reduce (or sometimes even remove) the need for additional support.

EHCPs: Key information for school leaders

Education, Health and Care Plans (EHCPs) are central to SEND provision, yet they remain one of the most misunderstood and inconsistently applied aspects of the SEND system. At their best, EHCPs provide long-term, legally enforceable entitlement to support tailored to the individual child's needs. At their worst, they're bureaucratically delayed, poorly written or inadequately delivered. To get it right, school leaders need more than a working knowledge – they need confidence, legal awareness and the resolve to advocate for children even when the system is faltering.

What is an EHCP?

An EHCP is a statutory document issued by a local authority under the Children and Families Act 2014. It sets out a child's special educational needs, the provision required to meet those needs and the educational outcomes they're working towards. It also includes information about health and social care where relevant.

Under Section 37 of the Children and Families Act 2014, the LA must ensure the special educational provision specified in an EHCP is made. This isn't optional, advisory or aspirational – it is a legal obligation. Provision described in Section F of the EHCP must be delivered in full, and the outcomes in Section E should form the focus of teaching, planning and review.

You may have a lot of students in your setting who will qualify for an Education, Health and Care Needs Assessment (EHCNA). This is the formal process a local authority uses to decide whether a child or young person needs an EHCP. It looks at their needs across education, health and social care and at whether what they require goes beyond what a mainstream setting can ordinarily offer.

Sit down with your SENDCo and work on a priority list, as it's better for two people to have ownership of those difficult decisions. Where parents/carers are waiting, ensure clear information is given on how they can apply themselves.

Top Tip

It's also worth remembering that the school's view on whether a pupil is likely to receive an EHCP is irrelevant to a parent's right to request an EHCNA. Parents/carers can apply by themselves at any time so you should always point them towards your LA's process for doing so.

EHCP tribunal appeals: the scale of the problem

- In 2022/23, HMCTS tribunals recorded 14,000 registered SEN appeals — an increase of 24 per cent on the previous year (HMCTS, 2023).
- In 2023/24, that figure rose again to 21,000 — a further 55 per cent increase, the largest single-year rise ever recorded (HMCTS, 2024).
- By 2024/25, HMCTS recorded 20,000 outcomes in relation to SEN appeals, an increase of 19 per cent on 2023/24 (HMCTS, 2025).
- The success rate for families is extraordinary. In 2022/23, 98 per cent of decided cases were found in favour of the appellant (HMCTS, 2023).
- In both 2023/24 and 2024/25, that figure stood at 99 per cent (HMCTS, 2024; 2025). LAs are, in effect, losing almost every case they choose to defend.
- The financial cost is equally striking. Special Needs Jungle estimates that local authorities were allocated £153 million of resources in 2023/24 to defend tribunal appeals and that since the SEND reforms were introduced in 2014, the cumulative total stands at approximately £580 million (Special Needs Jungle, 2024).

Key takeaways for schools and parents

The patterns are hard to ignore. Appeals are rising rapidly and now affect roughly one in 40 EHCP decisions. Families are winning the overwhelming majority of cases, which tells you something pretty significant about the quality of LA decision-making. Yet local authorities keep spending public money defending cases they almost never win. What this means for schools is straightforward: evidence matters.

Who should lead the process?

While Section 36(1) of the Children and Families Act 2014 makes it clear that anyone can request an EHCNA (including a parent, carer, young person or any professional), in practice, this is the role of your SENDCo. It's part of the SENDCo's statutory responsibilities under the SEND Regulations 2014, which require them to coordinate provision and advise on the graduated approach. It's neither appropriate nor sustainable for individual teachers to lead this work, even if they're concerned about a particular pupil's needs.

A robust, school-led application is far more likely to be successful. This includes:

- a full graduated response with clear evidence of assess, plan, do, review cycles
- costed provision maps showing exactly what the school has already put in place under SEN support
- standardised assessment data, teacher observations and pupil voice
- contributions from relevant professionals (e.g. SaLT, EP, CAMHS), ideally with reports that clearly outline the child's difficulties and their impact on access to learning.

However, legally, the threshold for an EHCP is actually relatively low. Under Section 36(8) of the Children and Families Act 2014, an LA must secure an EHCNA if the child or young person *may* have special educational needs and it *may* be necessary for special educational provision to be made for them. This 'may/may' wording is deliberate and important, because it doesn't require certainty or proof at the point of request, only the possibility. It's a point often misunderstood or misrepresented by LAs during the early stages of the application process.

Therefore, technically, you should be able to write an EHCNA quite quickly and submit it. However, due to demand, it's better to include as much evidence as possible at this stage as you want yours to stand out. Beware though: some authorities have been somewhat 'over-enthusiastic', shall we say, with what they want the evidence to look like. This list of expectations is likely not legally binding, as CAFA law trumps what the Code of Practice says, so *always* do your homework with the legality of their expectations.

Issues arise when schools fail to support their SENDCo in building this evidence base. Requests for assessment can be refused on the grounds that the school has not yet done enough to meet need from its own, very limited resources (see the SEND Code of Practice, paras 9.14–9.16).

The assessment and plan process

Once a request for an EHCNA has been submitted, the LA has six weeks to decide whether to proceed with the assessment (SEND Code of Practice 9.17). If they agree, the full process from request to issuing a final EHCP must be completed within 20 weeks, unless exceptions apply (SEND Regulations 2014, Regulation 13).

Authorities regularly fall short. My son's EHCP timeline was significantly over legal time frames. Having achieved 17 EHCP successes in the past five years with a 100 per cent success rate, I've seen how it's more difficult than ever. My top tips are to be prepared to hassle the LA over their timeframes and inability to adhere to the law, and be prepared to take it further. Also, encourage parents to use the ombudsman complaints system. We all need to work together to send the message to local government and beyond that these delays are unacceptable. Complaining to regulatory bodies assists with this.

Following assessment, if the LA agrees to issue an EHCP, the plan must:

- Be specific and quantified. Vague terms like 'access to support' or 'regular check-ins' aren't acceptable under law.
- Specify the means, frequency and responsibility for each provision.

The legal test (as established *in L v Clarke and Somerset County Council* [1998] ELR 129) is that provision must be so specific and clear that there's no room for doubt as to what is to be provided, by whom and when.

School leaders (but by default, the SENDCo) must ensure that class teachers are aware that the EHCP outcomes and the provision specified aren't optional.

They form the statutory core of that student's educational entitlement. Provision must *not* be diluted or substituted without formal review or amendment. If you're not meeting everything in Section F, go back to the LA for more money or request specialist provision where appropriate.

Funding and banding

Most LAs use a 'banding' system to determine the level of funding attached to each EHCP. However, it's important to note that this system is not referenced in the legislation. What matters legally is whether the provision described in Section F is delivered – not whether it fits within a particular funding bracket.

If the funding is insufficient to deliver the specified provision, the school must seek additional 'top-up' funding (commonly known as Element 3 funding). This is usually done through the local funding panel and requires:

- detailed costed provision maps
- evidence that the existing delegated funding (Element 1 and 2) has already been exhausted
- data showing that outcomes aren't being met despite current provision.

CAFA and the SEND Code of Practice (9.77–9.79) both make it clear that it's the LA's duty to secure provision, not the school's responsibility to absorb the shortfall. Schools shouldn't be subsidising statutory provision from their core budget.

When mainstream isn't the right fit

If a pupil's needs cannot be met in a mainstream setting, even with an EHCP, the school must not simply 'manage' the child until a placement breaks down. Proactive evidence-gathering and partnership with parents is essential.

Under Section 39 of CAFA, parents have a right to request a particular school or type of provision, including special schools and units. If the school agrees that specialist provision is appropriate, this should be documented through:

- professional advice (EP, SaLT, SEMH or autism specialists)
- long-term evidence that mainstream strategies have not met need
- a formal review of the EHCP with recommendation for specialist placement.

It's vital to maintain high-quality, documented provision while this process is ongoing. Withdrawing support in the hope of 'proving' that the setting isn't suitable isn't only unethical, it could also be used against the school in tribunal.

If the LA refuses to assess or issue

LAs sometimes refuse to assess, or assess but then decline to issue a plan. In these cases, the parent or young person has a right of appeal to the First-tier Tribunal (Special Educational Needs and Disability). While technically the appeal is the family's, the school plays a vital role in preparing evidence, attending hearings and supporting the process. I've heard of LAs suggesting that schools can't attend but there's no legal reason not to when you're an advocate for the family and if they want you there.

If a plan is issued but is inadequate (e.g. with vague wording, missing provision or no measurable outcomes) the school should support the family in challenging it. Many LAs rely on school staff not having the time, expertise or appetite for a legal battle but when schools stand firm, they can be powerful agents of change.

Some LAs ask SENDCos to write outcomes. This legally is not their job, so bat it back to the LA. You can, as a school, suggest amendments post annual review, which can be added in. Also, annual reviews don't *need* to be annual. You can chuck an extra one in at any point when needs aren't effectively met. Keep being a (professional) nuisance to get what's needed for your pupil (then multiply that by all the pupils you need to do this for).

Your responsibilities

EHCPs cannot be left to the SENDCo alone. Governors, heads and senior leaders have statutory and ethical duties to understand, support and oversee this area of provision. Specifically:

- know your legal duties under the Children and Families Act 2014, SEND Regulations 2014 and SEND Code of Practice
- back the SENDCo with dedicated time, administrative support and access to professional development, as well as backing any legal challenges to your LA
- challenge inadequate EHCPs and refuse to implement poorly written plans that lack specificity or don't reflect the child's actual needs

- ensure provision maps and costings are live, regularly updated and accessible to leadership and governors
- keep high aspirations, but recognise that national benchmarks like ARE may not reflect a child's EHCP outcomes. Personalised progress matters most.

EHCPs aren't just useful to have, they're a legal right. Done well, they enable long-term, meaningful access to education and better life chances. But they demand robust knowledge, tenacity and a willingness to wade through bureaucratic nonsense to do what's right. Leadership has an important role in overseeing the constant pressure that's needed to secure outcomes.

The importance of not having a one-size-fits-all approach

We know that we can't apply a neat, consistent system to every pupil. Schools rely on structure to function, but increasing needs mean increased flexibility. When it comes to pupils with SEND or additional needs, uniformity in approach can quickly become a barrier rather than a support.

Every pupil is an individual, with a unique combination of strengths, difficulties and context. We can maintain high expectations and uphold whole-school values without insisting that all pupils travel the same path to meet them. Flexibility isn't about lowering standards, it's about giving pupils what they need to reach them. Thoughtful adaptation, whether it's in behaviour management, communication or curriculum access, is what inclusion really looks like in practice. Supporting pupils individually doesn't mean letting go of consistency; it means embedding equity into your consistency.

Part 3

Building relationships with key staff

17 Strengthening SEND through relationships

A well-written SEND policy matters, but its success ultimately depends on the people who implement it. In every school, it's the strength of relationships between leaders, SENDCos, LSAs, class teachers and wider pastoral staff that determines the quality of provision for students with SEND.

SEND leadership is never a solo endeavour. Yet many SENDCos feel isolated, even if you, as their senior leader, don't share that view. Whether you're leading a small primary team or working across departments in a secondary setting, strong working relationships are essential. This means clarity around roles and responsibilities, and communication that is purposeful, professional and underpinned by mutual respect.

In this section, we'll explore how to foster a relational culture that enables inclusive practice to thrive. From establishing a shared vision to supporting your SENDCo in a strategic role, I'll offer practical insights into how effective relationships strengthen SEND provision across your whole school. No doubt, as you're working towards a highly inclusive school, you're already embedding many of these strategies.

The human side of inclusion

As school leaders, we must resist reducing inclusion to a checklist. Inclusive practice is essential, but it's also complex, time-consuming and emotionally demanding. It takes immense skill to manage a classroom while mentally tracking who needs visual prompts, who mustn't sit near the door, who won't speak aloud today, and who needs to be noticed every 20 minutes or they'll drift away completely.

Think back to your own classroom teaching. I remember believing each new seating plan would be the plan to end all plans. We'd live happily ever after until July. Alas, I was never right. There were never enough corners for my particularly 'fizzy' classes. Each new plan brought new issues! But changing it every few weeks was excellent for building a classroom community.

Ultimately, this part of the book is about recognising the sheer scope of what we ask teachers, SENDCos and support staff to do – and offering empathy, realistic systems and meaningful support. You can't build a truly inclusive culture if staff feel they're constantly failing, or worse, failing alone.

As we explored in Part 1, reasonable adjustments must genuinely be reasonable. That means creating environments where staff can speak up without stigma. The definition of 'reasonable' must reflect your staffing, training and the real constraints of the classroom. Teachers are committed professionals who will do everything they can but they need permission to be honest about what's manageable.

The scope of the job

It's easy to talk about inclusive practice in abstract terms: 'We need to meet every child's needs.' 'We must personalise learning.' 'High-quality teaching for all.' You've likely heard these statements from stakeholders. All true. All necessary. But zoom in from the strategic to the classroom level, and the reality can be overwhelming. Each of those statements translates into hundreds of individual actions.

In many classrooms your teachers aren't supporting one or two children with additional needs, they're juggling multiple. They're adapting for students with autism, ADHD, speech and language difficulties, sensory needs, anxiety, undiagnosed profiles and more... simultaneously, and often with limited support.

I've been that member of staff crying in the cupboard weekly, plate-spinning a class with around 33 per cent SEND, with no leadership back up, and working in a MAT that was brutal. It sucks. I questioned my career choice on a daily basis. When you add in the paperwork, parent liaison, meetings and intervention groups, it's no wonder teachers are exhausted. That's before we even mention differentiation, assessment or teaching the rest of the class.

Personally, I've always maintained that I can work in any school as long as the SLT supports me as an individual and has my back. It's staff culture and relationships that keep people in their roles and that, in turn, lower recruitment and retention issues.

That said, from a headteacher's perspective there are times when staff expect the moon on a stick. It can be difficult to judge whether you're being supportive enough, but I think supporting yourself should be high on your agenda.

Top Tip

If you're not already in a school leader network where you can ask advice anonymously in areas such as this, I can recommend Head Teacher Chat (https://headteacherchat.com).

Wellbeing

I run a Facebook group – *The Sweary SENCo* – to support staff juggling the impossible whilst still trying to be kind to everyone (including themselves). There's also a SENCo SOS button on my website if you ever need a bit of impartial advice about workload or wellbeing, or contact me if you want a chat about your school context.

As both a teacher and consultant, I've written extensively about SEMH and staff wellbeing. I'm not one for fluffy self-help clichés. Baths and mindfulness apps might help a bit, but most of our stress comes from inadequate systems, toxic expectations and impossible workloads. Wellbeing is about control, boundaries and making peace with the hard choices we sometimes have to make. Especially in education, where martyrdom is practically built into the job description.

SENDCo life brings extra complications. It's an isolating role. You're not part of a year group or team that sees you daily. When I was a class teacher, colleagues would notice if I was struggling. As a SENDCo, you can quietly unravel in your office without anyone clocking it. That's why I always say: *tell someone*. I've had major life events where I told my Head – not because I needed anything to change, but so someone knew. If I burst into tears over a dodgy provision map, there'd be context.

When the issue *is* school-related, it feels even trickier. That's where peer networks come in. If your home life is solid, use that space to decompress. If not, jump online in my group. You can ask anonymously, and chances are someone's faced the same challenge and lived to tell the tale (with union advice if needed).

Ultimately, staff wellbeing *isn't* a luxury – it's the foundation. Happy staff = happy children = excellent progress.

18 Building a relationship with your SENDCo

If you've ever been a SENDCo yourself, you'll know this truth: there's never, ever enough time. Of course, time is short in every school role, but it's increasingly recognised that SENDCos are drowning. Many speak of constant scrutiny, overwhelming workloads, and the emotional toll of being the go-to person for everything from EHCPs to crisis support.

The role is meant to be strategic, yet it's often consumed by reactive tasks: chasing paperwork, supporting LSAs, calming dysregulated pupils and managing last-minute transitions. Many SENDCos still teach, some full-time. Others are given a fraction of the time needed to lead SEND provision effectively. Add in the emotional labour of being the sponge for distressed teachers, parents and students and it's no wonder that burnout is rising.

In my *Sweary SENDCo* article series, burnout is a recurring theme. Each week in my Facebook group, I ask: 'What's made you a sweary SENDCo this week?' and it's consistently the most popular post. The issues range from being an emotional punching bag to battling with the LA and everything in between. As a school leader, you'll likely recognise some of these frustrations.

Mr P Does ICT, a well-known teacher voice online, describes SENDCo-ing as 'the hardest job in the school'. So with this in mind, ask yourself:

- Does your SENDCo have the time and status to lead strategically?
- Are you checking in regularly — not just when there's a crisis?
- Have you considered succession planning, coaching or admin support to ease their load?

Understanding roles on paper is very different from building the trusting, collaborative relationships needed to make this work in practice. This is where you, as the school leader, make all the difference. If you want inclusive practice to flourish in your school, you have to invest not only in strategies, but in the people leading them. That starts with understanding the full scope of the SENDCo role and building a working relationship built on trust, clarity and shared vision.

What your SENDCo wants you to know

Through my research, conversations in SENDCo networks, and the *National SENCo Workforce Survey: Time to Review 2018–2020* (Boddison, Curran and Moloney, 2021), several consistent themes emerge about what SENDCos need from their school leaders. These insights may sound simple but, when enacted well, they can transform how effective – and sustainable – your SENDCo's work becomes.

The role is bigger than you think

Despite being a statutory role, the sheer breadth of your SENDCo's responsibilities is often underestimated. They're not just writing provision maps and attending annual reviews: they're coordinating external agencies, supporting SEMH interventions, managing EHCP compliance, leading CPD and often line-managing LSAs or inclusion teams. Many are also teaching, acting as DSL or sitting on SLT. Even highly capable SENDCos can't do it all without support.

Between 2018 and 2020, primary SENDCos saw their allocated time increase by just 18 minutes per week; secondary SENDCos by 54 minutes. By 2020, that put primary SENDCos at an average of 2.15 days per week and secondary at 2.32 days, despite rising EHCP caseloads, increasing emotional need and the mounting pressures of the pandemic period. The survey found that 55 per cent of primary and 70 per cent of secondary SENDCos still weren't being given enough time to do their job effectively (Boddison, Curran and Moloney, 2021).

They need their profile raised

SENDCos are school leaders. They hold legal responsibility and play a vital role in the lives of vulnerable children. Yet many feel invisible to staff and parents. Whether that's perception or reality, you can help by:

- including your SENDCo in SLT meetings, even just the start, to respect their time
- publicly valuing their input in briefings or newsletters
- ensuring they present at INSET or CPD sessions on inclusive teaching
- encouraging them to lead or co-lead whole-school inclusive strategies, not just SEND
- asking for their views publicly and promoting their expertise.

Research from 2020 found that two thirds of SENDCos were not on SLT and a primary SENDCo was twice as likely to be on SLT as their secondary counterpart

(Boddison et al., 2020). If you want SEND to be everyone's responsibility, your SENDCo needs the platform to lead it.

They need support, not just goodwill

One statistic that really stood out to me is the lack of administrative support available to SENDCos. In primary schools, 85 per cent of SENDCos had no dedicated administrative support for a role that is arguably among the most administratively demanding in the school. In addition, around 90 per cent had no deputy or assistant SENDCo (Boddison, Curran and Moloney, 2021). Secondary schools fare better on both counts, but not by enough, and the need for structured admin support is growing across all phases. Without protected non-contact time, SENDCos are pushed into reactive crisis mode. Bath Spa University's best practice guidance recommends:

- one full day per week of protected non-contact time as a baseline
- additional time proportionate to school size and EHCP numbers
- dedicated admin support, to avoid wasting expertise on formatting minutes or uploading documents.

My own research goes a step further and considers the increasing demands of the last few years and the increasing need for even more release time (See blog links on companion website). SENDCos with structured time and admin help report significantly higher job satisfaction and effectiveness.

They need to network

SEND leadership is complex and ever-changing. SENDCos benefit from external networks but often struggle to attend due to lack of cover or leadership not seeing the value. You can support this by:

- allowing your SENDCo to attend LA network meetings or national conferences
- building regional collaborations across schools, especially within your MAT
- encouraging CPD that includes leadership coaching or mentorship
- offering paid time or time off in lieu (TOIL) if networking happens outside the working day.

External engagement keeps your SENDCo sharp, connected and less isolated. Yes, some events feel like a waste of time. But mostly, local cluster groups are invaluable – a space to decompress and compare notes. A nose around another school beats a Zoom meeting (where I may also be checking emails while listening). As a school leader, I'd encourage you to get out of the building for network meetings too. If it's in a coffee shop? Embrace it. Lose the guilt. You and your staff deserve it.

They need a CPD budget

Many SENDCos report having no allocated CPD budget, yet they're expected to stay up to date with national policy, legal changes and developments across autism, SEMH, dyslexia, ADHD and SLCN. I know from my own work that many SENDCos pay for subscriptions and webinars out of their own pockets. Providing a dedicated CPD budget (even a modest one) shows you value their professional development. Better still, agree that it can be used for leadership development too. It's a small step that sends a big message: their growth matters.

Ask them what they need

Every school context is different, but firefighting is a consistent theme. The simplest way to support your SENDCo well? Ask. Some useful conversation starters:

- 'What's taking up most of your time right now and could someone else help with it?'
- 'What's something you've wanted to do in your role but haven't had capacity for?'
- 'Are there any quick wins that would help ease your workload?'
- 'Do you feel you have enough influence over school-wide decisions about inclusion?'

Consider flexible working

Your SENDCo's role is increasingly strategic, requiring focused time for report writing, provision mapping, responding to consultations and ploughing through EHCP paperwork without interruption. Trying to do all of that at a school desk with a queue of LSAs, teachers and students needing immediate support is challenging, to say the least. A day at home now and then, or a set afternoon each week, creates breathing space for the deep work that drives long-term impact.

Allowing flexible working within reason signals trust and professional respect. The DfE has also encouraged schools to explore flexible working options for teachers, and this is a low-cost, high-impact step in that direction (DfE, 2024). We're not talking about going fully remote: just the occasional planned day or weekly half-day where strategy can breathe without distraction.

Creating a culture where inclusion is everyone's responsibility

SEND provision should never rest on one person's shoulders. The SENDCo coordinates. The teachers deliver. But it's you, as the school leader, who enables or blocks the culture in which those roles thrive.

For teachers to feel empowered – not burdened – by inclusion, your SENDCo must be positioned as a trusted partner, not a compliance officer or an add-on. This begins with the messages you send. When you talk about SEND at staff meetings, do you speak in terms of shared responsibility? Do you create time for joint planning, modelling or peer support? Do you highlight successes and celebrate professional curiosity? When you get this right, your SENDCo becomes someone teachers actively seek out because they feel supported, not scrutinised.

It is also important to recognise inclusive teaching as a staff wellbeing issue. When teachers feel safe to ask for help without judgement, they are far more likely to sustain good practice. Conversely, when they feel overwhelmed and left to 'just get on with it,' burnout becomes inevitable. As a busy teacher, I know what it's like to sit through another initiative at a staff meeting and inwardly roll your eyes. That's why it's vital to help your staff see how inclusive and adaptive practices can actually make their lives easier, not harder.

You must actively create a culture where it is normal and encouraged for teachers to:

- flag concerns early without fear of blame
- access informal support from the SENDCo or inclusion team
- reflect openly on what's working and what isn't
- see SEND as a shared priority, not an additional burden.

I've been guilty of doing too much in every job I've had, especially starting out. When you begin at full tilt, it quickly becomes the expected norm. It's not sustainable. So when you welcome a new member of staff, remind them: don't work yourself into the ground trying to prove your worth.

It's also worth having a candid conversation with your SENDCo about this. Even if you consider yourself an excellent collaborator, we all have blind spots. Creating space for honest dialogue is the first step towards strengthening your school's inclusive culture. A downloadable Leader's Reflection Checklist is available on the companion website.

How much time should a SENDCo have?

The pressures have only grown. More complexity. More tribunals. More time-consuming paperwork. But still, in many schools, no more time or support to do the job. If you're reading this and thinking, yes, that sounds like our SENDCo then it's time to ask: what are you doing differently now, compared to five years ago?

For extended tables and guidance on recommended release time based on school size and SEND profile, see the companion website.

SENDCo pay: a time for reflection and fair recognition

My national survey (2023) of 1,201 SENDCos showed striking variation in how this statutory role is remunerated. While 343 respondents are paid on the leadership scale – reflecting the strategic scope of the role – others are on significantly lower arrangements:

- 248 receive the SEN allowance only, without a TLR or leadership pay
- 234 are paid on TLR2, often considered the minimum threshold for substantial additional responsibility
- just 43 receive TLR1, despite the whole-school nature of their duties.

This variation may stem from historical arrangements, school size, funding constraints or differing views on what constitutes appropriate pay. It's a complex picture, and school leaders are often doing their best to balance equity and budget in incredibly tight circumstances. Still, it may be time for a review.

What does the national picture suggest?

SENDCos who aren't on the leadership scale should almost always receive a TLR, given their statutory duties: leading SEND strategy, coordinating provision, advising colleagues, working with parents and external agencies, and ensuring compliance with CAFA and the SEND Code of Practice. These responsibilities clearly meet the TLR threshold and in many cases TLR1 may be more appropriate than TLR2, especially where line management or strategic oversight is involved.

It's also worth noting that the SEN allowance wasn't originally intended for SENDCos. It's typically awarded to teachers working directly with a high proportion of students with complex needs in specialist settings. While some SENDCos may have inherited this arrangement, it was never designed to recognise the strategic, whole-school nature of the role.

A prompt for school leaders

If you haven't reviewed your SENDCo's pay recently, now might be a good time. This isn't about catching anyone out, it's about ensuring your pay structures reflect the vital, and increasingly complex, work your SENDCo does every day. Consider:

- Is your SENDCo leading whole-school SEND strategy?
- Do they line-manage staff, oversee EHCPs and liaise externally?
- Are they on a pay scale that reflects this scope and accountability?

Many school leaders are already doing the right thing. Where adjustments aren't immediately possible, having an open conversation about how your SENDCo's role is valued can go a long way. It's not always about the money – though let's be honest, it's also the main reason we work – it's about professional respect, recognition and sustainability. We all want to retain talented SENDCos. Reviewing pay in line with national expectations is one important way to help make that happen.

Reflection questions for classroom teachers

- **What types of needs am I most frequently adapting for in my classroom?**

- Where do I feel confident making reasonable adjustments? Where do I feel less sure?
- Do I feel comfortable asking for help with SEND support? If not, what's getting in the way?
- When was the last time I spoke with the SENDCo about a specific child's provision or my classroom setup?
- How do I take care of my own wellbeing when supporting students with complex needs?
- Do I feel confident adapting lessons to meet a range of needs? Where would I like more support?
- When I face a barrier with a student's learning or behaviour, do I feel comfortable discussing it with the SENDCo or a colleague?
- Do I feel I'm 'doing it alone', or part of a team when it comes to SEND?
- What small changes could help me feel more supported in delivering inclusive practice?
- When I seek help for a student, how is that perceived – by others, and by myself?

19 Best practice for working with LSAs

LSAs and HLSAs are often the quiet drivers of inclusive practice, working across classrooms, intervention spaces and nurture rooms. But the educational landscape grows more complex, it's worth revisiting how we deploy, support and develop our LSA teams to make the best use of their skills, sustain their wellbeing and maintain consistency across the school.

The Education Endowment Foundation's (EEF) guidance report *Deployment of Teaching Assistants* (2025) is essential reading on this topic. It doesn't critique LSAs themselves, but highlights the need for systems that support them effectively... and that's where leadership comes in. The report's recommendations centre on:

- training and CPD that reflects the complexity of the role
- clear structures and line management to support wellbeing and consistency
- regular communication and inclusion in planning cycles
- strategic deployment based on pupil need and staff expertise.

When schools take the time to structure their LSA provision well, the benefits are clear: improved pupil outcomes, stronger staff retention and a shared sense of ownership over SEND and inclusion. Crucially, it also protects the professionalism of LSAs — many of whom already give far more than is asked of them every day.

Carving out specific LSA roles to meet different types of need is both smart and sustainable, especially as the demands on SEND provision continue to grow. The following section explores three key roles: intervention, pastoral and SENDCo admin support, with clarity and respect for the many schools already thinking in this way.

Specialist LSA roles

In schools with growing SEND cohorts and more complex needs, the traditional model of assigning LSAs to individual students or classrooms often becomes unworkable. Many schools are moving towards a more strategic deployment model, where LSAs hold specialist or semi-specialist roles that meet broader needs – while still maintaining a child-centred ethos.

There's no one-size-fits-all structure, but having specialist roles within your LSA team helps distribute responsibility, ensures coverage and reduces reliance on 'floating' support that lacks focus. Importantly, it allows team members to build confidence and expertise in particular areas, which supports both impact and retention.

Intervention Specialist LSA

This role focuses purely on the delivery of structured, evidence-informed interventions, such as:

- literacy and numeracy catch-up programmes
- speech and language packages (e.g. NELI, Talk Boost)
- working memory or processing interventions
- precision teaching and pre/post-teaching support.

Why it works: consistency of delivery leads to better pupil outcomes; progress can be tracked more robustly when one person is accountable for implementation; and class teachers are freed up from juggling group withdrawal and in-class differentiation simultaneously.

Key considerations: this LSA should be trained and monitored regularly, with a clear intervention timetable. Their role should include liaison time with the SENDCo and class teachers to review impact. They may also support assessments, data tracking and resource development related to the interventions they deliver.

Line managed by: SENDCo or inclusion lead.

Pastoral/Regulation Support LSA

This role focuses on SEMH, behaviour, regulation and daily transitions. Key duties include:

- supporting children through transitions, break and lunch times, or difficult moments

- co-regulation and calming support (e.g. walking breaks, sensory strategies)
- supporting in-class behaviour management or 'check-in' systems
- running social skills groups.

Why it works: this role provides a known adult for children who are emotionally vulnerable, creates a predictable, relationship-based model that reduces escalation and is often the linchpin of inclusive practice across the school.

Key considerations: this role may overlap with ELSA-trained staff or wellbeing mentors, depending on your staffing model. It should be coordinated with your DSL or behaviour lead.

Line managed by: SENDCo or DSL.

SENDCo Admin and Provision Support LSA

Perhaps the most underused but impactful support role is one that focuses on the administrative burden of the SENDCo, which, let's face it, has grown exponentially. As noted earlier, over 85 per cent of primary SENDCos have no admin support, despite spending hours on paperwork, records and meeting notes that pull them away from strategic work. Key responsibilities might include:

- organising and updating provision maps and SEN records
- preparing paperwork for annual reviews or referrals
- managing the SEN inbox and triaging communication
- creating intervention timetables and staff rotas
- supporting the SENDCo in data analysis and resource preparation
- being present at the start or end of the day for parental catch-ups
- supporting monitoring of intervention impact and gathering feedback.

Why it works: it frees up the SENDCo to lead rather than just manage; helps maintain accurate records for audits and inspections; and keeps the SEND office running smoothly during busy periods (e.g. EHCP review season).

Key considerations: this may be a term-time admin role rather than a classroom-based post and should be graded appropriately. Some schools combine it with exam access arrangements coordination or EAL support, depending on context.

Line managed by: SENDCo.

In short, when you move beyond the 'LSA per child' mindset and think instead about building a team with roles and specialisms, you unlock far more sustainable, impactful provision – and we do it in a way that protects everyone's capacity, wellbeing, and sense of purpose.

Top Tip

Whilst the 'Velcro LSA' model – where an LSA is assigned to shadow a single pupil closely throughout the day – isn't ideal for promoting independence, it's absolutely fine, necessary even, when you're supporting children with complex needs who've been placed in mainstream without adequate specialist provision. If it's about pupil wellbeing and safety, stick with the Velcro.

Reflection questions

- Do your LSAs have a clear focus, or are they pulled in multiple directions?
- Would any of your existing team thrive in one of these more structured roles?
- Could a small restructure improve provision *and* reduce SENDCo workload?
- Are your pastoral and academic supports balanced and well-coordinated?

20 Supporting your SENDCo to lead

With all this in mind, it's worth considering how to help your SENDCo lead in this area of LSA line management and other leadership considerations. Many SENDCos arrive in post via the route marked 'excellent classroom practitioner with a big heart'. What they generally haven't been handed is a ready-made toolkit for line-managing adults, challenging colleagues' practice or running performance management reviews (PMRs).

If you want SEND to sit at the heart of school improvement, you have to back your SENDCos with explicit leadership development – not just more paperwork. The new NPQ should support this better than the old NASENCO (don't get me started on that but I hear there are still gaps!).

Give them a leadership mentor – not just another course

- Pair them with an assistant or deputy head who can model agenda-setting, difficult-conversation etiquette and data-driven decision-making.
- Arrange shadow days: budget meetings, pupil progress, staffing panels. Seeing the process demystifies it and means fewer panicked 'What's FTE again?' emails later.
- Keep it reciprocal: ask your SENDCo to brief your SLT on inclusion data trends – a confidence-builder and a win for collective insight.
- Ensure it's needs-led – plan with your SENDCo. It may also be that other members of your leadership team need some CPD to work on their people skills.

Structured CPD: coaching, NPQs and bite-size leadership

The NPQ for SENDCos replaced the NASENCO award and became mandatory for all new SENDCos from September 2025. It's an 18-month programme with a much stronger emphasis on whole-school SEND leadership rather than just operational management.

At the moment, the overall feel around the new NPQ for SENDCos is quite mixed. On paper, it's seen as a more accessible, practical, leadership-focused qualification that's funded and designed to fit around workload, which many people welcome. Informally, people are also describing it as still not as practical as hoped, with questions about quality, impact and whether it will genuinely improve SEND provision or just add another layer without fixing the real issues like workload and lack of protected time.

Planning ahead: consider your SENDCo's time out of class, SLT mentoring and how the NPQ might affect your CPD budget. If your current SENDCo already holds the NASENCO, they won't be expected to retrain.

For full details on NPQ funding, delivery and assessment, see the companion website.

Clarify line-management structures in writing

Your LSA team needs clear structures. Create three simple documents:

- LSA team structure chart – who answers to whom, when and for what.
- Performance cycle calendar – dates for goal-setting, mid-year check-ins and PMRs.
- Delegation matrix – which decisions your SENDCo can make alone and which need SLT sign-off. Stick these on the wall (and on Teams or Drive) so everyone's aware. You can download templates from the companion website.

Support data analysis

Leading adults means proving impact. Offer your SENDCo:

- access to MIS analytics (SEND progress, attendance, behaviour data), plus half-termly slots with your data manager to set up dashboards and discuss trends
- a working day per half-term explicitly for strategic SEND leadership – no gate duty, no firefighting; just time to prepare reports, PMR evidence and training plans.

Rehearse the difficult conversations

Role-play isn't just for Year 2 drama lessons. Schedule practice for calling out inconsistent differentiation, giving constructive feedback to an LSA whose intervention hasn't moved the dial, or challenging a colleague who's 'parking' a student outside the classroom.

Short, safe rehearsals build muscle memory and reduce 3am worry cycles. This won't work for everyone, of course. I hate role-play with a passion, possibly due to emotional scarring from my NPQH assessment, when I was given an incorrect brief and the actor I was paired with hadn't a clue what I was talking about. We both rolled with it; I survived and received an apology. Either way, some form of training in holding people to account in a nurturing way is useful for all leaders, not just your SENDCo.

Make PMRs a joint venture to start with

You may wish to support your SENDCo by:

- providing a template aligned with LSA standards and school priorities
- co-observing at least one LSA session together and modelling objective note-taking
- sitting in on your SENDCo's first PMR as silent backup – then debriefing afterwards.

I was left to wing PMRs when I became an assistant head – I think they went OK; no one cried, at least. In hindsight, some support would have made them more effective.

Protect their seat at the table

Finally, leadership is as much about perception as skill. Ensure your SENDCo:

- presents at every SLT meeting, even if just a five-minute update
- leads a staff-meeting slot at least once a term on an inclusion priority
- represents your school at LA SEND forums or trust inclusion boards.

Visibility breeds authority and trust and signals to everyone that SEND is a whole-school, whole-leadership priority.

Ensuring adequate budgets

One of the clearest ways to demonstrate your commitment to inclusion is through training. Not just a twilight session or two, but a properly thought-through, ring-fenced, year-on-year plan that provides development opportunities for every part of your team.

SEND doesn't sit in isolation so neither should the CPD. I've seen many schools that have, understandably, prioritised core curriculum and safeguarding CPD in recent years. SEND CPD is an investment, not a quick win. To support learners to make better progress, the foundations of adaptation and learning in areas such as SEMH are key for all children. You might not reap the benefits straight away, but you'll certainly reap the long-term benefits exponentially compared to the usual 'sticking plaster' approach. I know school leaders are torn. In their hearts they're doing what's right for the children, but day-to-day pressures make this increasingly difficult.

Top Tip

Even a modest ring-fenced SEND CPD budget, agreed at the start of the year, sends a powerful message to your SENDCo and LSA team. It says their professional development matters, not just their output.

What to fund — and for whom

SENDCo	National conferences, ongoing CPD across all areas of SEND, legal updates, mental health, leadership, supervision, NPQs, LA negotiation, EHCP processes
LSAs/HLSAs	Intervention training (with fidelity), regulation strategies, trauma-informed practice, ELSA, specific SEND condition training
Teachers	Adaptive teaching, scaffolding strategies, SLCN/AAC approaches, in-class regulation support, writing SMART targets, IEP development, practical inclusion strategies
Governors	Strategic inclusion leadership, SEND governance responsibilities, understanding SEND funding, asking effective questions
School leaders	Strategic inclusion leadership, SEND tribunals, managing parental conflict, placement planning, LA negotiation, EHCP processes, supervision and coaching

Cost-effective, high-impact training opportunities

Here is a list of affordable or free SEND CPD opportunities that are well respected and widely used.

Provider	Offer	Cost	Best for
NASEN membership	Webinars, SENDCo updates, resources and legal briefings	Free (basic) or premium version available	SENDCos, teachers
Whole School SEND (via SEND Gateway)	Webinars, guides, audits and CPD packs	Free	All staff
EEF Guidance Reports	CPD guides on SEND, literacy, LSAs and behaviour	Free	Teachers, SLT
National College	Online accredited courses, some school-wide licences available	Varies	All roles
Positive Young Minds and The Sweary SENCo	Practical online SEND CPD, yearly CPD subscriptions and wellbeing support	Varies	Whole school, but mainly SENDCos
Local authority/ Teaching School Hub	Regular SEND networks, EHCP training, Early Years CPD	Often free or subsidised	SENDCos, LSAs
Virtual School/ LAC Services	Trauma, attachment and regulation training	Free	All staff
EDPsychs/ EdPsychEd	EP-led online courses and supervision packages	£50–£200	SENDCo, LSA, SLT
MAT/trust internal CPD	Custom SEND leadership, line management and governor updates	Often included	SLT, governors

SENDCo supervision: a strategic investment in leadership and wellbeing

We talk a lot in education about safeguarding supervision for DSLs, clinical supervision for therapists and coaching for headteachers. Yet SENDCos, who juggle some of the most emotionally and ethically complex decisions in the building, are still too often left to process it all alone.

Schools are catching up, and I've seen a marked increase in schools and trusts wanting supervision-style coaching for their staff. I've had very positive feedback from the trusts I work with; it really does make a difference. If you don't have any coaching or supervision yourself either, then get some.

In reality, SENDCo supervision isn't a luxury. It's a vital piece of professional care that helps your inclusion lead stay emotionally well, strategically focused and genuinely supported in what can be an isolating role. I have a SENCo SOS button on my website which comes through to my WhatsApp, and I regularly hear from SENDCos who feel they have nowhere to turn. Having someone outside school to look at things objectively is invaluable.

What is SENDCo supervision?

SENDCo supervision is a structured, confidential space for your SENDCo or inclusion lead to:

- reflect on their workload and emotional responses to challenges
- process complex or ethically difficult decisions – tribunal cases, placement breakdowns, safeguarding crossovers
- talk through systemic frustrations that can't be aired elsewhere
- develop clearer thinking around priorities, difficult conversations or conflicting pressures
- maintain boundaries, perspective and professional resilience.

It's about creating space for thinking, sense-making and decompression – with someone who understands the job.

Why every SENDCo needs this – and so do you

Supervision has long been embedded in health and social care – and for good reason. Leadership roles that carry responsibility for other people's lives, especially where trauma, systems pressure and emotional demand are high, require support structures that are proactive, not reactive.

SENDCos are navigating LA gatekeeping, supporting families through diagnoses and grief, advocating for children with escalating needs – often without adequate funding – managing LSA teams and staff conflicts, and feeling guilty constantly about what they haven't yet done.

All of this accumulates. Without the right outlet, it leads to burnout, decision fatigue and withdrawal from the role. You as a senior leader benefit too:

- a SENDCo who has supervision is more emotionally regulated and therefore more constructive in senior discussions
- it builds retention; many SENDCos cite isolation and lack of support as key reasons for stepping down
- it enables your SENDCo to process and contain staff and parental emotion more effectively, rather than carrying it around like a lead backpack
- it aligns with your staff wellbeing and workload policies – it shows investment, not just intent.

What should supervision look like?

Ideally, once every four to six weeks for 45–60 minutes, delivered by an external trained supervisor or a trained internal colleague but not their line manager. If it's to decompress about pupils, an internal supervisor works well; if it's more general, external is better, as it's difficult to discuss school or trust issues with a trust representative.

The agenda belongs to your SENDCo. Topics may include a case that's troubling them, relationships with staff or parents, role boundaries or their own wellbeing.

Done well, supervision is a space where, as one SENDCo put it: 'I can say the unsayable and be met with professionalism, not panic.'

It's also a safe place to celebrate wins – something that's often missing when you're the one quietly plugging gaps and putting out fires in the background.

Key benefits

- **Improved decision-making** – talking through difficult calls helps surface unconscious bias or blind spots before they become missteps.
- **Emotional literacy modelling** – SENDCos who receive supervision are better able to reflect on and model those skills in their own team leadership.
- **Whole-school gain** – the SENDCo often supports the emotional load of everyone else; giving them a space of their own increases the resilience of the whole system.
- **Another perspective** – if supervision is provided by an experienced SENDCo, there's plenty of empathy alongside practical ideas and signposting to strategies or resources.

Making it happen

You can contract an external supervisor. Many are former SENDCos, educational psychologists or SEND specialists. Consider cross-school or MAT arrangements if budgets are tight; group supervision for three or four SENDCos in a local cluster can still be highly effective.

Make sure your SENDCo knows this isn't a performance management tool – it's an investment in them, not just their outputs. If you already offer coaching or mentoring to leaders, add SENDCos to the list. Their need is just as great.

If you want to keep your SENDCo – and more importantly, help them thrive – give them what you'd want for your DSLs, your deputies and yourself: regular, structured space to think, feel and breathe. If you know this is an area for development at your school, discuss it with your governors to make it happen for all your key staff – and ideally for all staff at some point across the year.

Reflection questions

- Who currently supports your SENDCo, emotionally and professionally?
- Have they ever had the opportunity to offload to someone impartial?
- What would it say to the rest of your staff if SEND leadership wellbeing were made a visible priority?

21 Working with parents and governors

Working with parents

Working with parents of children with SEND is one of the most important and emotionally charged parts of a SENDCo or school leader's role. For many families, school hasn't been an easy journey. Some arrive at your door feeling let down, overwhelmed and exhausted from having to fight for every inch of support.

Building trust in that context takes more than coffee mornings and a copy of the SEND Information Report. It takes honesty, consistency, clear communication and the willingness to sit with discomfort when views differ. The hardest conversations I've had with parents have been in schools that didn't allow me to be fully transparent about what we could offer. Transparency is key and when it's compromised, relationships suffer. Those particular schools and I parted ways.

The foundations: trust and transparency

The best parent–school relationships are built on clarity and shared purpose. This means:

- being honest about what your school can and can't offer within existing resources
- explaining decisions clearly, with reference to the SEND Code of Practice – not just 'school policy'
- providing timely updates – not waiting until things go wrong
- ensuring parents don't hear good news for the first time in the EHCP review – celebrate success, however small
- ensuring parents don't hear bad news for the first time in the EHCP review – regular communication means no negative surprises.

You don't need to over-promise or perform. Most people value straight answers, especially when they've been on the SEND treadmill for a while.

One thing worth raising: be welcoming to families with children who have EHCPs. I've spoken to parents who've been actively put off applying to certain schools because, during the open day, the head or SENDCo stated outright that they couldn't meet need. Of course, there are some students who require a specialist setting, and there are circumstances where that conversation is appropriate. But many of these were pupils who would have been welcomed with open arms in schools I've worked in and who would have become valued members of the community. I strongly believe that with the right resources and funding, which is the LA's statutory duty, we can support the vast majority of children in mainstream. It's heart-breaking for parents to feel that a school doesn't want their child.

Navigating the difficult conversations

There will be moments when families and schools disagree – sometimes fiercely. This is often about provision type (mainstream vs specialist), or what should be in place now versus what can realistically be provided.

Parent view	School view	What helps
'My child needs a specialist school now'	'They are making progress here, and specialist would not meet current criteria'	Use data, targets and EHCP wording to evidence progress. Clarify LA thresholds for placement changes.
'Why isn't there a full-time 1:1 LSA?'	'A 1:1 would reduce independence and isn't what's recommended'	Refer to EEF guidance and Code of Practice principles, and explain why targeted adult support is more effective.
'Nothing is working'	'Interventions are in place, but outcomes take time'	Share provision maps, review cycles and next steps. Validate emotion, but stay focused on facts.
'Other schools have more'	'We're doing what we can within our resources'	Avoid comparison traps. Be specific about what's in place and how it meets this child's needs.

Top Tip

If it feels like a difficult conversation is coming, don't wait for it to escalate. Pre-empt it with a review meeting framed around shared problem-solving which changes the dynamic entirely.

Parents seeking more – or less – than what's needed

A common tension in SEND work is managing cases where parents either seek specialist placement that doesn't currently align with the pupil's needs or EHCP evidence, or actively resist formal assessment or an EHCP application, even when school feels it's essential.

When families want more than is warranted:

- Avoid positioning your school as the barrier. Instead, explain that specialist provision must match demonstrable need and outline how you're currently meeting it.
- Use LA descriptors or graduated response frameworks to demonstrate how the child fits or doesn't fit current thresholds.
- Offer a review cycle: 'Let's monitor over the next two terms and meet again with updated evidence.'

Remember that even if you don't think an EHCNA is warranted, parents may still be entitled to apply. Explain that their child may not be at the top of the priority queue – you may have five or more EHCNAs to progress – and agree a priority order with your SENDCo. You can offer to support parents in applying themselves, which is especially important where parents have additional needs of their own. This is a tough call; you are, to some extent, making decisions that shape children's futures. But the legal entitlement is clear.

The same applies to referrals. If a parent wants a referral for ASD or ADHD, support them and fill in the forms. Many children – especially girls – are falling through the net, having masked well at school but still carrying significant needs. They may become school avoiders or struggle unnecessarily as a result of being missed. We are not qualified to make these clinical judgements, so refer and let the qualified people decide.

When families don't want to 'label' or assess:

- Acknowledge fears around stigma or exclusion – don't dismiss them.
- Reassure parents that an EHCP is about entitlement and support, not diagnosis.

- Keep a clear record of school efforts to support the child and invite families to remain involved even if they initially decline assessment.
- In rare but serious cases, where a refusal to engage results in significant unmet needs, this may constitute educational neglect. If so, discuss with your safeguarding leads – social care involvement may be necessary.

Practical strategies that help

- Offer structured review meetings at least termly, with notes shared in writing afterwards.
- Provide a named point of contact – often a pastoral lead or lead LSA – who knows the child well.
- Make sure parents understand key documents: the provision map, SEN support plan, EHCP sections and the graduated response.
- Use visuals where possible – flowcharts, timelines and provision diagrams help families navigate the system.

Top Tip

If a parent relationship feels like it's deteriorating, act early. A brief, informal phone call to check in – before it becomes a formal complaint – can reset the dynamic entirely. Most parents respond well to being contacted when things are going right, not only when there's a problem.

Above all, approach every conversation with curiosity and compassion. Most behaviour from parents stems from fear – fear that their child will be missed, misunderstood or left behind. With many of the children I've supported, I can't begin to imagine what daily life looks like for that family.

When you lead with transparency and genuine partnership, even difficult conversations can become productive ones. When you show parents that you see the whole child, not just the paperwork, you create the conditions for trust. Not every family will agree with every decision, but they'll remember how you made them feel: heard, informed and included.

Reflection questions

- Do your SENDCo and SLT have a shared script for managing parental expectations?
- Are review meetings framed as collaborative?
- Do your staff feel confident having firm but fair conversations – or are they avoiding them?
- How do you ensure consistent communication when a child is supported by multiple teams?

Working with governors: making the most of your partnership

Governors can be a brilliant asset when it comes to SEND and inclusion if you know how to bring them on board. Too often, I've seen governors who want to help but aren't sure how, and school leaders who treat governor meetings as a tick-box exercise rather than an opportunity for genuine strategic partnership. Let's change that.

Keep them informed, not overwhelmed

Governors don't need to know every detail, but they do need a clear picture of your SEND priorities, progress and challenges. Regular, concise updates with clear headlines, key data and a quick summary of actions keep them engaged and ready to support. What works well:

- termly SEND reports in a consistent format: numbers, provision overview, impact data, current challenges and resource needs
- one-page summaries for each governor meeting; save the detail for those who want to dig deeper
- visual data where possible – graphs showing SEND progress versus whole-school performance, intervention impact and EHCP timeline tracking.

What doesn't work:

- drowning them in acronyms and jargon
- only contacting them when you need something (usually money)
- assuming they understand educational terminology
- presenting problems without context or proposed solutions.

Invite their strategic input

Governors are there to hold your school to account and that includes SEND provision. Encourage them to ask thoughtful questions about funding, staffing and the impact of interventions. Their fresh perspective can spot things you might miss and if you're fortunate, some will have knowledge of SEND themselves.

Good questions for governors to ask:

- How do we know our SEND provision is making a difference?
- Are there patterns in which children aren't making progress?
- What's preventing us from meeting needs more effectively?
- How does our SEND spend compare to similar schools?
- What are the warning signs we should watch for?

Share these questions with your SEND link governor – or better still, work with them to develop a set of questions tailored to your school's context and priorities.

Build relationships

Take time to get to know your governors, especially the SEND link governor. Share successes and struggles honestly; it builds trust and makes your work feel visible and valued. Invite your link governor to visit during the school day to observe interventions, meet LSAs or sit in on a review meeting (with parental permission). Share the human stories whilst maintaining confidentiality. Governors connect with 'Amira's made six months' progress in phonics' far more than statistics alone. Be honest about challenges; governors can't help if they don't know what's really going on. When something works, celebrate it together.

I've worked with some fantastic SEND link governors over the years. One came for a full day of our provision mapping session because she wanted to understand how we track provision. That level of engagement is gold standard but you have to build the relationship first.

Top Tip

Invite your SEND link governor to one meaningful event per term (a provision map meeting, an intervention showcase, a parent review), rather than waiting for the formal governor visit. A governor who truly understands your provision is a far more effective advocate.

Provide training and resources

Governors aren't mind-readers. Offering briefings or signposting accessible SEND information helps them understand the landscape and make informed decisions – and shows you're invested in a genuine partnership.

Training options include:

- governor induction to SEND – an hour covering the basics: what SEND is, the Code of Practice and your school's approach
- annual SEND update – changes in national policy, LA updates and what they mean for your school
- external training – many LAs and teaching school hubs offer governor SEND training
- joint sessions with another school – cross-school governor training can be cost-effective and builds useful networks.

Resources to share:

- your school's SEND policy and Information Report, with a cover note explaining the key points
- NASEN's governor resources (www.nasen.org.uk)
- DfE guidance on SEND governance
- this book – well, the relevant sections at least.

Use them as advocates

Governors can champion SEND within wider school leadership and the community. When they understand the importance and complexity of SEND, they're more likely to back requests for funding, staffing or policy changes.

This is particularly valuable when making the case for resources – applying for additional funding, requesting extra LSA hours, defending SEND spending when budgets are tight – or when proposing changes to provision (such as setting up a nurture room) or challenging the LA over inadequate support or funding. A well-informed governor asking strategic questions in a finance meeting carries real weight. They're not staff with a vested interest – they're independent voices acting in the school's best interests.

Keep communication two-way

Don't just report upwards – ask for feedback, ideas and support. This turns governors from distant overseers into active allies. Questions to ask your governors:

- 'What would help you understand SEND provision better?'
- 'Are there areas where you'd like more detail – or less?'
- 'Do you have expertise or contacts that could support our SEND work?'
- 'What questions should I be asking that I'm not?'

Some governors have unexpected expertise – I've known governors who were educational psychologists, SEND solicitors, occupational therapists or parents of children with SEND. You won't know unless you ask.

Making it work in practice

The relationship between school leaders and governors around SEND works best when you're proactive – not waiting for a crisis – trust their judgement to challenge you constructively, value their time by making meetings efficient and purposeful, and see them as genuine partners rather than rubber-stampers.

If your current relationship with governors around SEND feels distant or difficult, start small. Invite your link governor for a coffee and a conversation about what they'd find helpful. You might be surprised how much changes when you approach it as a genuine partnership rather than an accountability exercise.

The power of teamwork

When you truly work with all your stakeholders – parents, staff, governors and beyond – the results can be extraordinary. It's that genuine partnership, built on trust and respect, that turns tricky challenges into shared victories.

You might look around your school and wonder whether you'll ever get there – whether the culture you want, the support every child deserves, is really within reach. It is. It never happens overnight, but small steps taken consistently add up quickly. Focus on the progress made whilst holding your inclusion vision in mind. In fact, a staff meeting asking everyone to design their own inclusive school utopia would be a revealing exercise.

Before long, those small moves become bigger strides, and one day you'll pause and look back, surprised at how far you've come. That's the real power of working together: creating a school where everyone feels seen, heard and valued – and where every child can thrive. So keep going. Keep building those bridges. Because when it works, there's nothing quite like it.

Part 4

Inspection, accountability and school improvement

22 The 'O' word: where SEND fits with Ofsted

If there's one thing that makes school leaders wake up at 3am in a cold sweat, aside from a broken boiler or the Wi-Fi going down, it's the word 'Ofsted'. It looms large in the school calendar, in SLT meetings and in the subconscious of even the most outwardly serene headteacher. But we also know that the main thing is doing right by the children, not just passing an inspection.

We should plan for the children, not for Ofsted. Always. If we get it right for them, we'll get it right for Ofsted anyway.

Say the word 'Ofsted' in a staffroom and the temperature drops a few degrees. My issue has never been with accountability itself; all school leaders want to improve their schools. The problems lie in how inspections can feel disconnected from the realities of schools, particularly when it comes to SEND. That said, there are genuine signs of progress in the framework, and schools that truly prioritise inclusion often find inspection validates rather than threatens their work.

This chapter covers what you need to know about the current framework, how to prepare authentically and, crucially, how to use self-evaluation to drive real improvement rather than just satisfy inspectors.

Top Tip

The best inspection preparation isn't a late-night document sprint. It's the culture you've built all year. If SEND is genuinely embedded in everyday practice, inspectors will see it, because it will be visible in every classroom, not just the SENDCo's office.

SEND at the core makes everything stronger

Schools that succeed with inclusion tend to be strong across the board. Inclusive practice, properly supported staff and children who feel understood all create an environment where learning can thrive. Parents feel listened to, children make genuine progress, and wellbeing isn't an add-on. These are exactly what inspectors are meant to value.

The shift towards authentic provision over impressive paperwork means that if you're already doing the right things for children, inspection should feel like recognition rather than performance.

The current framework and recent shifts

Since November 2025, Ofsted has been operating under a new inspection framework, and for schools doing good work on SEND and inclusion, the changes are broadly positive.

Single-word overall effectiveness grades are gone. In their place, schools receive a report card grading performance across eleven evaluation areas on a five-point scale: Exceptional, Strong standard, Expected standard, Needs attention, and Urgent improvement. Safeguarding is judged separately, as either 'met' or 'not met'. Crucially, inclusion is now one of those 11 areas in its own right, not just a thread running through the quality of education judgement. Inspectors will be looking explicitly at how well schools identify and support pupils with SEND and at outcomes for those pupils.

The inspection process itself has also changed significantly. Deep dives into specific curriculum areas have been removed. Instead, the lead inspector now has a substantive pre-inspection call with school leaders to discuss context, improvement priorities and key evidence. Inspectors then agree on focus areas aligned to the school's improvement plan, which makes the whole process more collaborative and less of an ambush.

The 2025 update to the joint Ofsted/CQC framework for local SEND provision also placed stronger emphasis on collaboration between education, health and care inspectors, a welcome recognition that children's needs don't fall neatly into one professional box. Inspectors are now expected to listen to the lived experiences of families, staff and children themselves, rather than relying purely on documentation.

There's also a sharper eye on data. If SEND pupils are over-represented in your figures for poor attendance, exclusions or underachievement, inspectors will want to understand why and what you're doing about it. That's not a threat; it's an opportunity to show the work you're already doing.

Ofsted has also proposed creating a national team of senior inspectors with specific SEND expertise, which would address the persistent and long-standing problem of inspectors arriving without sufficient knowledge to make well-informed judgements. Too many SENDCos have found themselves explaining EHCP basics or justifying why a child's sensory regulation strategy isn't 'poor behaviour'. A dedicated specialist team can't come soon enough.

What hasn't changed is what inspectors actually want to see: inclusion embedded in everyday classroom practice, not filed away in a policy document. They want to see that pupils with SEND access a full and ambitious curriculum, that adaptations are thoughtful and consistent, and that staff across the school, not just the SENDCo, understand and own their responsibilities.

Ongoing challenges

The reforms aren't without problems. Critics across the sector have raised concerns that the new grading model feels underdeveloped. Inspectors themselves report that training has been rushed, with over 27 hours of online content plus face-to-face sessions to absorb. Whilst pilot inspections and the Ofsted Academy aim to smooth the rollout, confidence across the sector remains patchy.

Sir Martyn Oliver, appointed Head of Ofsted in 2024, has warned schools not to exclude children with higher needs for the sake of performance tables, arguing that inclusion is central to school effectiveness. This aligns with what SENDCos know to be true, though translating aspiration into practice remains challenging given limited funding and chronic staffing shortages.

Even with framework improvements, problems persist:

- **Lack of specialist knowledge**. Many inspectors still lack the depth of training needed to make well-informed judgements about SEND. Misinterpretation of practice leads to inaccurate conclusions.
- **Personality-dependent outcomes**. How an inspection goes can depend heavily on which team shows up, something every leader I've spoken to recognises from experience.
- **Systemic barriers misunderstood**. Schools are judged on outcomes they can't always control. Resources rarely match the rhetoric of the SEND Code of Practice. Inspectors often assess provision against ideals rather than the lived constraints of staffing, funding and specialist access.
- **Real-world pressures ignored**. Even dedicated professionals struggle to produce the evidence inspectors expect whilst actually supporting children. The workload is relentless.

My Ofsted experiences

Having been through five Ofsted inspections across different frameworks, I can confirm the experience depends on a mix of factors. Some have been relatively positive; others far from it. In schools desperately needing improvement, we often found ourselves working overtime to paper over the cracks. Some inspectors are sharp enough to unpick things you don't expect them to notice, so don't give them any reason to dig deeper if there are issues you'd rather stayed buried. If you're proud of your school and its practices, you'll happily let them dig to their hearts' content.

I've had my share of horror stories. Having been both a SENDCo and assistant head, I know SEND was often treated as my sole responsibility, regardless of whether I had any authority over staffing or resources. In one school, I had no say at all in staffing decisions despite many classes being led by HLSAs, which caused significant issues across the board.

One inspection sticks with me. That week, I'd set up a carefully planned provision for children with speech and language needs: a morning hub with a bespoke curriculum I'd designed, delivered by an experienced LSA. The children were thriving. Then, whilst I was off because my son was unwell, the CEO walked around, decided they didn't like it and disbanded it immediately. Those children were sent back into their classes with no tailored support.

The following Monday, Ofsted called. During the walkaround, an inspector asked what provision was in place for a particular pupil. What could I say? There had been well-functioning, bespoke provision the week before; now it had been removed entirely. The child was sitting in a class led by an HLSA with no additional support. I found myself trying to explain the situation without throwing my school under the bus, even though I wanted to be very honest about what had just happened.

Moving forward: what needs to happen

Inspection needs fundamental rethinking. Instead of highlighting weaknesses and walking away, inspectors should be part of the improvement journey. If a school requires improvement, inspectors ought to share responsibility for supporting development, offering expertise, coaching and monitoring alongside critique. Accountability should not be detached from responsibility.

Schools that fall below the expected standard in any area will now receive support from new regional improvement teams, with budgets of up to £100,000 per school. This is a step in the right direction, but genuine collaborative accountability needs to go further.

What would make a real difference:

- **SEND expertise as standard.** A dedicated team of inspectors, trained by SEND specialists and experienced in specialist settings, would bring more consistency and credibility. Every inspection team should include at least one member with genuine expertise.
- **Clearer, more accessible reports.** Reports should be written so that parents can easily understand them, especially those navigating SEND systems. The move to report cards is a genuine opportunity to make inspection outcomes reflective of the lived school experience.
- **Recognition of systemic barriers.** Reports should clearly distinguish between school-level failings and wider structural issues such as lack of access to speech therapy or CAMHS delays. This would give parents an honest picture and reduce unfair pressure on schools.
- **Collaborative accountability.** If weaknesses are identified, inspectors should remain part of the journey, providing support and resources. Judgement and improvement should go hand in hand.

The human cost

Beyond frameworks and handbooks, there's the emotional toll inspection takes on staff. For SENDCos, the pressure is especially acute.

You're expected to know every detail about every child with additional needs and to articulate how provision links to progress and outcomes. Add in the constant juggle of meetings with parents, assessments and staff training, and inspection week can leave people utterly drained.

There's a particular stress in explaining SEND practice to inspectors who may not fully understand it. The sinking feeling when you realise an inspector has misinterpreted a child's behaviour, or doesn't recognise your strategies, is all too familiar. It puts staff in the uncomfortable position of having to advocate not only for children but also for the validity of their own professional expertise.

Ruth Perry's death highlighted the extreme strain inspections can cause, forcing a national conversation about whether accountability, as currently structured, is compatible with staff wellbeing. Whilst reforms have been promised, schools remain deeply aware of this legacy. Many colleagues still speak of 'inspection trauma', and it will take more than new report cards to rebuild trust.

Practical guidance: preparing authentically

- **Lead with integrity**. If every decision is guided by what's best for children, paperwork will naturally reflect authentic practice. Inspection then becomes validation of what you already do rather than an ordeal. This looks like policies that match daily reality rather than aspirational documents, support plans that staff actually use rather than impressive folders gathering dust, and evidence that emerges naturally from good practice rather than being created for inspection.
- **Stay informed.** Keep up to date with the evolving framework, report card categories and SEND-specific expectations. Share feedback where you can; schools' voices matter in shaping how inspection develops.
- **Advocate for your reality**. If inspectors lack specialist knowledge, don't shy away from explaining what effective SEND practice looks like in your context. Be clear about systemic barriers beyond your control, such as LA delays, therapy waiting lists or funding gaps.
- **Document strategically**. You don't need reams of paper, but you do need to show impact. Focus on clear provision maps showing what happens, when and why; progress evidence that tells the real story rather than just headline data; pupil voice showing children feel supported and are making progress; communication records with parents and external agencies; and evidence of staff training and how it has changed practice.
- **Push for partnership**. If your school is judged as requiring improvement, remind inspectors and yourself that recommendations should be the starting point for joint support, not the final word.

Top Tip

Before any inspection, brief your SENDCo on the three or four pieces of evidence that best demonstrate the impact of your SEND provision. Not a folder of everything; a confident, clear narrative of what you do, why you do it and what difference it makes.

Final thoughts on inspection

For now, the best advice is to focus on what matters most: creating an environment where every child feels safe, included and able to learn. If that's the heartbeat of your school, inspection becomes easier to withstand. Authentic practice holds up under scrutiny far better than short-term fixes designed for an inspector's visit.

The system is far from perfect. Underinvestment, inconsistency and gaps in inspector knowledge remain huge challenges, and many inspectors would admit this themselves. Schools deserve an inspection system that is genuinely supportive, consistent and properly informed about SEND. Until inspectors are as accountable for their judgements as schools are for their outcomes, there will always be a disconnect.

But change is underway, and with persistent pressure from the sector, there's an opportunity for Ofsted to move from being a source of anxiety to being a partner in improvement.

In the meantime, if you are living and breathing SEND, inclusion and wellbeing, you are already doing the most important thing. The rest, frameworks, gradings and shifting inspection models, are simply the backdrop to the real work: ensuring that individual children have the school experience they deserve.

The bigger picture: politics and systemic barriers

Ofsted doesn't operate in a vacuum. Its approach reflects broader political choices about accountability, funding and trust in schools. Whilst inclusion is celebrated in policy, many schools are expected to deliver high-quality provision in the face of squeezed budgets, long waiting lists for health services and chronic staffing shortages.

This creates a frustrating double bind: schools are judged on outcomes they can't always control, yet support for improvement is limited or inconsistent.

For SENDCos, the gap between policy and reality is especially stark. The SEND Code of Practice outlines clear entitlements for children, but resources rarely match the rhetoric. Inspectors, meanwhile, often assess provision against idealised standards rather than the lived constraints of staffing, funding and access to specialists. This mismatch leaves schools penalised for systemic failings far beyond their control.

I've been asked more than once why a pupil isn't receiving everything outlined in section F of their EHCP. Sometimes it's because the plan is out of date and no longer reflects the child's current needs; other times, it's due to delays or shortfalls from the local authority. I always make sure I have the email trail showing our attempts to secure funding or provision. It's become a necessary part of the job.

Inspectors occasionally arrive with fixed ideas about what inclusion should look like and get hung up on impractical expectations, such as why we don't pre-teach every subject for every child with SEND. We could, of course, extend the school day by a few hours to accommodate that. I hope you can feel my eyes rolling.

Another systemic issue is the one-size-fits-all nature of the inspection framework. Mainstream schools with a handful of SEND pupils face very different challenges to special schools with highly complex cohorts. Yet the same framework is often applied with minimal adjustment. Until Ofsted develops more nuanced models that reflect these differences, schools will continue to feel unfairly judged.

Reflection questions

- Does your current SEND provision reflect genuine everyday practice, or has it been shaped around what looks good on paper?
- How confident is your SENDCo in talking to an inspector about the impact of your provision?
- If an inspector spoke to your pupils with SEND, what would they say about how well they're supported?
- Are there systemic barriers affecting your outcomes that you could articulate clearly and evidence honestly?

23 School self-evaluation and improvement

Self-evaluation done well is a chance to pause, reflect and identify what's working and what needs attention. The process should be honest and constructive, not an exercise in self-criticism. I've developed comprehensive self-evaluation tools that schools can adapt; what follows is a brief overview of the key areas. Contact me for the detailed, trackable version.

Leadership and vision

What to look for

Leaders setting the tone for inclusion. When leaders actively champion SEND and model inclusive values, it becomes part of the school's DNA rather than something bolted on.

- **Governors asking the right questions.** Governors who engage with data, provision and pupil voice around SEND demonstrate that oversight is a genuine commitment to equity.
- **Consistency across policy and practice.** Strong leadership ensures policies aren't just documents on a shelf but are clearly visible in classroom practice and staff decision-making.

Teaching and learning

What to look for

Clear differentiation and adaptation. Lessons should offer scaffolds where needed but never cap ambition. The goal is access and challenge, not one or the other.

- **Support strategies visible in classroom routines.** Inclusive teaching is most effective when strategies such as visual supports, retrieval practice and scaffolding are built into everyday learning, not added as afterthoughts.

- **Teachers who can explain their approaches.** Staff who understand the 'why' behind their strategies show that inclusive practice is informed, deliberate and research-based.

Outcomes and progress

What to look for

Assessment data that tells the real story. Schools should be able to show progress in terms of learning, independence and confidence, not just headline results.

- **Interventions making measurable difference.** Good evaluation means knowing when an approach works and being confident enough to stop what doesn't.
- **Pupil voice showing genuine progress.** Hearing pupils talk about their own progress, whether academic or personal, is one of the strongest indicators that provision is working.

Wellbeing and inclusion

What to look for

Calm, positive classrooms. Behaviour systems should focus on understanding and support rather than sanctioning children for difficulties linked to SEND.

- **Supported staff.** When staff wellbeing is prioritised, they are better placed to support pupils consistently and effectively.
- **Engaged parents.** Parents should feel like partners in the process, not passive recipients of information. Regular communication and involvement in decision-making are key.
- **Early intervention systems.** Schools that intervene early and proactively are far more successful than those relying on reactive crisis management.

Continuous improvement and professional development

What to look for

- **Whole-staff and targeted SEND training.** Training needs to be relevant, ongoing and accessible for all staff, not one-off sessions that don't embed.
- **Staff who can articulate changed practice.** Real impact is shown when staff can describe the difference training has made to their daily work with pupils.
- **Regular review built into the improvement cycle.** Evaluation should not be a once-a-year exercise but part of ongoing reflection and adjustment.
- **A culture of curiosity.** Improvement thrives where staff feel safe to take risks, trial strategies and learn from mistakes.

The role of the local authority

When reflecting on school improvement, it's important to look beyond the school gates. The effectiveness of your LA and the quality of your working relationship with it can have a direct impact on outcomes for children. Are they responsive to requests for statutory assessments? Do they provide timely and appropriate support services? Are they transparent in communication and consistent in decision-making?

Schools should be able to evidence how they work with the LA, whether through minutes of meetings, joint planning documents or examples of effective collaboration around EHCPs. Equally, if there are barriers or gaps in support, it's important to record these too. Being able to demonstrate both the strengths and the challenges of your LA relationship shows that you are reflective, proactive and honest about the wider context in which your school operates.

Reflection questions

- Looking honestly at your self-evaluation, which of the five areas is your school's greatest strength, and which needs the most attention?

- How regularly do you gather pupil voice specifically around SEND provision, and how does it inform your improvement priorities?
- Is your LA relationship working well for your pupils? If not, what's one concrete step you could take to improve it?

Part 5

Case studies

Case studies

Case studies bring theory to life. For school leaders, they provide a window into the realities of practice, showing how challenges unfold in real time and, importantly, how schools can respond. No two pupils are the same, but what these examples demonstrate is that with creativity, persistence and collaboration, even the most complex situations can be turned around.

The following case studies highlight how small adjustments, thoughtful strategies and strong partnerships with families can make a lasting difference. They are not just stories of individual children; they are illustrations of what is possible when school leaders commit to inclusion and refuse to give up.

We hear from two real schools, followed by an anonymised secondary case study, a set of marginal-gains examples from individual pupils, and three SEMH case studies. Together, they show inclusion not as a policy goal but as something schools are doing, every day, under real constraints.

Brays School - Kari Anson, Headteacher

Brays and Forward Education Trust are driven by inclusivity. This approach is rooted in equity, recognising each child may require different resources and strategies; the goal is to provide an environment where all children can learn and communicate effectively.

Why it matters

The total communication approach demonstrates that inclusion in a special school context means ensuring every child has a means of expression, whatever form that takes. When schools get this right, children are heard, valued and truly listened to.

Total communication approach

Brays uses a holistic communication strategy that accommodates a wide range of communication needs. In practice, this means:

- individual symbols for children who can comprehend and use them as a means of communication

- full communication books for those who can engage with more complex systems
- Makaton used alongside verbal communication across the school day
- Big Mack buttons for children who cannot speak, enabling participation in activities such as morning greetings
- auditory scanning books and Etran frames for children who use eye movements to communicate.

Multi-agency collaboration

Staff work closely with speech and language therapists, occupational therapists and physiotherapists and visual and hearing impaired specialist teachers to ensure communication strategies are appropriately designed and regularly reviewed.

Ongoing development

Continuous professional development keeps staff knowledgeable about best practice in inclusive education and communication. Regular feedback from children, parents and professionals is used to refine approaches, ensuring provision remains responsive to individual needs.

Inclusivity at Brays is not merely about providing equal resources; it is about recognising and addressing the unique needs of each child. By combining a total communication approach with genuine multi-agency collaboration, every child is supported to find their voice and thrive.

Inspire Partnership - Kyrstie Stubbs, Deputy CEO

Being an inclusive school should be a given. For me, it has always been about creating a sense of belonging in all my schools, where everyone feels included and celebrated. It should never be an afterthought; it should be at the heart of every decision we make as leaders.

SEND support across all our schools centres on it being a responsibility of all staff. It runs as a thread across everything we offer our pupils.

Why it matters

The Inspire Partnership model shows what is possible when a trust takes a genuinely system-wide approach to SEND. Rather than relying on individual SENDCos working in isolation, the hub model creates consistency, capacity and professional headspace across schools.

Therapeutic environments

One of the most effective changes we made was developing therapeutic environments where children feel safe and secure. Low-stimulus classrooms and corridors, combined with a commitment to reducing cognitive load in all displays, have had a significant impact on both concentration and self-regulation. This supported not only our most vulnerable pupils but the whole school community.

From interventions to adaptations

Our approach to interventions has changed completely. When I started in this role, I was clear that inclusion was not about taking children out of lessons; that approach was adding to the problem. By changing how we structured lessons, using dual coding consistently across every subject, changing the background colour of slides and reducing the number of words on screen, we began catering for the needs of all pupils all of the time.

We still take children out of lessons for what we now call 'outerventions' for specific support, often addressing specialist areas in EHCPs, but these are far less frequent. The majority of pupils now receive their adaptations within their lessons.

Bespoke pathways for higher-need pupils

Many of our schools have now developed bespoke pathways for children who would ordinarily have attended specialist settings, but for whom there are not enough places. My view is that they are our children, regardless of where we feel they should be placed. These pathways have been carefully developed as individual curricula meeting high need effectively.

This hasn't been without challenges. We've needed to invest time in developing these pathways and in training dedicated staff to deliver them. In a world of reducing budgets, this has at times felt impossible. But the progress we've seen has been worth the short-term difficulty. Where children previously needed a 1:1 ratio, the setting and curriculum now better meet their needs, and we've been able to reduce that ratio.

Parent communication

A significant barrier to inclusion centres on parent partnerships. Where families don't fully understand processes and systems, it can cause unnecessary anxiety and misunderstandings. We've worked hard to develop communication channels with parents: newsletters specifically for families of children with SEND, regular meetings with SENDCos, and information leaflets covering all systems and processes. These are all recorded for parents who struggle to read, and translated into our key community languages across the trust.

Hub leadership model

One of the changes that made the biggest difference across our schools was a structural shift: moving away from a SENDCo in each school towards a hub model, with leaders responsible for SEND across a number of schools. SENDCos no longer feel pulled in two directions, neither their best class teacher nor their best SENDCo. They now have the headspace and time to do the job well.

This has also enabled consistent approaches and assessment systems. For example, we now have a programme for EAL pupils joining our trust, where all schools implement a six-week programme created specifically to accelerate language acquisition.

Advice for schools that are struggling

Work backwards. Think about the ideal: what would your provision look like at its best? Then think about which parts you can do now with planning and focus, what you could do if you thought creatively about budget and EHCP funding, and what you need capital or further support to achieve.

Making your school a place where everything you do is done with SEND pupils in mind will inevitably support all your pupils.

Whitefield Primary School - Marie Beale, Deputy Headteacher & Inclusion Manager

At Whitefield Primary School, we seek to be more than just a school; we want to be a family for our children. In a recent Ofsted inspection, a child told the inspector we were 'a place of hope'. We are located in one of Liverpool's most challenged and diverse areas.

Why it matters

Whitefield shows what is possible when a school in one of the most deprived areas in England decides that context is not an excuse. High attendance, strong outcomes and a genuine culture of belonging are achievable even when families face significant adversity, if the school's values are lived rather than laminated.

Context

Our school sits in an area ranked in the bottom one per cent nationally on the Income Deprivation Affecting Children Index (IDACI). A large majority of pupils are eligible for free school meals and pupil premium funding. Many children arrive with significant barriers to learning. Our approach, developed in partnership with our families, is to ask 'what does each individual need and what has happened to them?' rather than adopting a deficit model of 'what is wrong with you?'. We want all our children to leave feeling able to stand proud among their peers. We are proud to have attendance and assessment outcomes well above national averages.

Values and vision

Our ethos is simple but powerful: to ensure every child is content, regulated and ready to learn, regardless of ability, background or need. We say 'we value each child for who they are and prepare them for who they can be', and 'be here, be you, belong'. Staff welcome children back after an absence with 'we really missed you' and 'how can we help you catch up?' Reducing anxiety and encouraging attendance starts with those small acts of connection.

Environments are carefully designed to reduce distractions and cognitive load: visual timetables for all, routines such as 'three good things' built into the day to promote wellbeing.

A growth curriculum

Alongside the more traditional foundation curriculum, we have developed what we call a 'Growth Curriculum', focused on life skills, attitudes and tools that help children succeed whatever their background. We place a strong emphasis on oracy and vocabulary development, weaving rich language experiences into every lesson. Reading runs as a fundamental thread throughout the school. Technology is used to break down barriers to learning and enhance accessibility for all pupils.

Wellbeing and environment

We are a Gold Level Attachment and Trauma Sensitive school and hold the Carnegie Gold Mental Health Award. Many of our children have experienced adverse childhood experiences. Staff have had extensive training over the last decade to look beyond behaviour and ask 'what has happened to this child?' We use survey data to identify and support pupils' mental health needs, and we extend this support to families, recognising that a child's wellbeing is inextricably linked to their home environment.

A parent programme focused on co-regulation supports families to work in partnership with us. Extended daily play sessions of 30 minutes, including activities such as silent discos and mud kitchens, promote positive social interactions and build relationships with staff. For our older children, classrooms have been redesigned to be neutral, comfortable and stripped back, with varied seating and workspaces. Pupil voice consistently highlights the positive impact these environments have on learning and wellbeing.

Overcoming obstacles

We face significant financial and space challenges as a Private Finance Initiative (PFI) school. We actively seek out grants, run projects, collaborate with other schools and forge partnerships to enhance our resources and expertise. We are outward-facing, always looking for new ways to improve and share our practice. We welcome numerous school leaders each year and actively share our expertise at conferences and in publications.

A mainstream secondary: thriving through inclusion against the odds

This large mainstream secondary serves an inner-city community with significant challenges. Over 40 per cent of students are eligible for free school meals, and mobility is high, with new students joining throughout the year. Many families face unstable housing, low incomes and limited access to external services. SEND needs are above national averages, with a particularly high proportion of students identified with social, emotional and mental health (SEMH) needs, as well as speech and language difficulties.

Why it matters

This case study shows that high-performing SEND provision is possible in the most under-resourced settings, but only when leadership makes it genuinely non-negotiable and responds creatively to the gap between what the system should provide and what it actually delivers.

Culture from the top

Despite these barriers, the school has developed a culture where inclusion is non-negotiable. The headteacher is clear: 'If we don't get it right for our most vulnerable learners, then we aren't getting it right at all.' This ethos has filtered through every level of leadership. SEND is discussed not only in SENDCo meetings but at senior leadership briefings and governor panels, ensuring accountability is embedded across the school.

Staff development

Teachers are supported to take responsibility for all students in their classrooms. Every member of staff receives regular training on adaptive teaching, with a focus on trauma-informed practice and executive functioning strategies. The school has invested in developing subject specialists as SEND champions, so staff have colleagues they can turn to for practical advice in their own departments.

The skills hub

One of the biggest challenges has been the shortage of external agency support: speech and language therapy input is minimal, and CAMHS waiting lists are lengthy. In response, the school established a 'skills hub' staffed by highly trained support assistants. The hub provides short, targeted daily sessions in vocabulary, working memory, self-regulation and social communication. These sessions are closely planned with subject teachers so that strategies feed directly back into classroom learning. The hub also doubles as a safe space for students who need to regulate, helping to reduce disruptive incidents.

Timetabling for belonging

The school has taken creative steps with its timetable. Rather than withdrawing students from lessons they enjoy, interventions are scheduled during less critical slots, ensuring students continue to feel part of their peer group. Every intervention is designed to be short, sharp and purposeful, so that time away from the main curriculum is minimised.

University partnerships

Financial pressures remain a daily reality. To maximise resources, the SENDCo has built strong partnerships with local universities, creating placement opportunities for trainee educational psychologists and speech therapists. This not only boosts provision but provides valuable real-world experience for trainees.

Impact

Attendance for students with SEND has risen steadily over three years. Exclusions have dropped significantly. Attainment gaps are closing, and GCSE progress measures for the SEND cohort now sit close to national averages, a major achievement given pupils' starting points.

The strongest evidence comes from the students themselves. Pupil voice surveys show that students with SEND feel listened to, respected and supported. One Year 11 student summed it up: 'This is a place where people understand how I learn. They don't make me feel different; they make me feel like I can do well.'

The SENDCo is reflective about the journey: 'We haven't solved every challenge. Funding is always tight, and external services remain stretched. But what we can control is the culture of our school, and that's what drives everything. Inclusion is not something we do; it's who we are.'

Marginal gains: small changes, significant impact

In education, it's often the small, thoughtful adjustments that create the biggest impact. Known as marginal gains, these are the tiny changes that may not seem dramatic in isolation but, when combined, can completely change a child's school experience. A supportive word, a change in routine, or a targeted piece of mentoring can tip the balance from disengagement to progress.

The following examples show how marginal changes made a meaningful difference to individual children.

- *Maya (primary)* found transitions between lessons difficult, leading to frequent dysregulation. Her learning mentor created a simple visual timetable she could carry with her. Having clear visuals gave her reassurance, and her stress levels noticeably reduced.
- *Ben (secondary)* struggled with anger management and often ended up outside lessons. A learning mentor started a daily ten-minute check-in, simply asking how his morning had been. This consistent relationship gave him an outlet, and the number of incidents dropped.
- *Kirsty (primary)* found maths overwhelming and felt she could never keep up. Her teacher introduced the 'one more minute' strategy, allowing a little extra processing time before moving on. She began completing work she had previously abandoned.
- *Daniel (secondary)* rarely contributed in class discussions and was often overlooked. A teacher began asking him the first question in small-group work, making sure it was something he could answer confidently. Over time, Daniel's contributions grew and he started putting his hand up in whole-class sessions.
- *Leila (primary)* had suffering attendance due to low confidence. Her learning mentor agreed to meet her at the gate each morning and walk in with her. This five-minute act made her feel safe and valued, and her attendance steadily improved.
- *Sophie (primary)* struggled with writing tasks and often gave up before starting. A teacher introduced a simple writing frame with sentence starters. Within weeks, Sophie's confidence grew and she began producing full pages of writing independently.

- *James (secondary)* found homework overwhelming and rarely handed it in. By agreeing that he could submit shorter pieces focused on quality over quantity, he began turning in work regularly and felt proud of his progress.
- *Ella (primary)* was anxious about reading aloud. Her teacher arranged for her to practise with a trusted friend before whole-class sessions. This small adjustment reduced her anxiety, and she now volunteers to read during group work.
- *Hannah (secondary)* had dropping attendance because mornings felt chaotic. Staff gave her early access to the building so she could arrive quietly and calmly. This small routine helped stabilise both her attendance and her confidence in lessons.
- *Tom (primary)* often left the classroom without permission when frustrated. A teacher gave him a time-out card he could use to request a short break. He began using it appropriately, and incidents reduced dramatically.
- *Leanne (secondary)* struggled with written exams due to slow processing speed. Allowing her extra time and use of a laptop made the difference between failing and passing, and boosted her motivation to keep trying.
- *Amira (primary)* found it difficult to join playground games. A teaching assistant introduced her to a peer buddy system, and within days she was playing happily with others. This improved both her friendships and her engagement in class.

SEMH case studies

Sometimes the challenges schools face with pupils who have significant social, emotional and mental health needs can feel overwhelming. Behaviour logs stack up, exclusions seem inevitable, and staff can begin to feel that the issues are simply too big to resolve. Yet, with dedication, patience and the right support, schools can help even the most complex situations improve.

The following three case studies show how, by working closely with families, offering consistency and tailoring provision, schools were able to turn things around for pupils who were otherwise on the brink of exclusion.

Nathan (Year 9)

Why it matters

Nathan's case shows what happens when a school looks past behaviour and asks what's driving it. A multi-agency, relationship-centred response, rather than an escalating sanctions cycle, kept a vulnerable young person in education.

Nathan presented with frequent outbursts in class, poor attendance and defiance towards staff. His behaviour records showed multiple suspensions and he was at serious risk of permanent exclusion. Teachers described him as disruptive and disengaged, but conversations with his family revealed a recent parental separation and significant instability at home.

What the school did

- A multi-agency meeting was held, bringing together the pastoral lead, learning mentor, SENDCo, family support worker and parents.
- A bespoke support plan was created, giving Nathan access to a safe space and a trusted adult he could go to when he felt overwhelmed.
- A temporary reduced timetable was put in place, with one afternoon per week in the inclusion unit focusing on emotional regulation and social skills.
- Staff were trained to use restorative conversations rather than punitive detentions, helping Nathan to rebuild relationships.
- His parents were supported with parenting workshops and given regular feedback so they felt included rather than blamed.

Outcome

Over the course of a term, serious incidents reduced significantly. Nathan began to re-engage with his core subjects and his self-confidence grew. By the end of Year 9 he was on a full timetable again, with exclusion no longer under consideration.

Aisha (Year 10)

Why it matters

Aisha's case illustrates how a change in approach, driven by one advocate within the school, can shift the trajectory entirely. Suspensions were not solving the problem; a personalised, relationship-based plan did.

Aisha had a history of trauma and presented with extreme anxiety, verbal aggression and regular refusal to attend lessons. She was well-liked by peers but often became the focus of conflicts. The school had issued multiple fixed-term suspensions, and her attendance had dropped below 70 per cent.

The turning point came when a new SEMH coordinator was appointed and advocated for a different approach.

What the school did

- Aisha was allocated a key learning mentor who checked in with her twice daily and acted as a consistent point of contact.
- A graduated approach was applied: staff identified her triggers, reduced transitions and allowed her to begin lessons in a calm space before joining the main class.
- A personalised curriculum was agreed, including vocational subjects she was motivated by, such as hair and beauty.
- The school worked closely with her family through fortnightly meetings, ensuring strategies were consistent at home and at school.
- While waiting for CAMHS support, the school provided in-house counselling sessions.

Outcome

Within months, Aisha's attendance rose to 90 per cent. Exclusion was no longer under discussion, and she began working towards qualifications that felt meaningful to her. Teachers noted a marked decrease in confrontations, and her family expressed gratitude that the school had not given up on her.

Oliver (Year 6)

Why it matters

Oliver's case is a reminder that behaviour labelled as SEMH is sometimes masking something else entirely. The SENDCo's decision to look deeper, rather than manage the surface, changed the course of this child's education.

Oliver joined a new school in Year 6 with a history of frequent outbursts. Staff initially believed his behaviour was driven by poor emotional regulation; he often shouted, stormed out of lessons or became withdrawn. Exclusions had been threatened at his previous school, and he arrived with very low self-esteem.

The SENDCo decided to dig deeper. Through observation and careful conversations with his teachers and family, they noticed that Oliver struggled most when asked to explain his thinking or join in discussions. A referral was made to speech and language therapy, and assessment revealed significant language processing difficulties that had previously gone undetected.

What the school did

- Targeted SaLT strategies were introduced in class to simplify language and give Oliver more processing time.
- A small-group intervention focused on language comprehension and expression was put in place.
- Staff training helped the whole team recognise when behaviour was masking communication difficulties.
- The SENDCo coordinated a successful EHCP application.

Outcome

By the end of Year 6, Oliver's behaviour had stabilised and he had clear, tailored support in place ready for his transition to secondary school. This case highlights the importance of looking beneath the surface of behaviour and recognising that what appears to be SEMH may in fact be unmet communication needs.

The thread running through every case study in this section is the same: when leaders and staff commit to understanding each child, refuse to give up and are willing to be creative, the results speak for themselves. Inclusion is not a policy. It is a practice, built in small decisions every single day.

Reflection questions

- Looking across these case studies, which resonates most with challenges your school currently faces?
- Where in your school are the 'marginal gains' waiting to be made? Who could identify them?
- Do your staff feel confident looking beneath behaviour to ask 'what is driving this?'
- Which of these approaches could you implement next term, without additional resource?

Final reflections

Leading on SEND is hard. It's a marathon, not a sprint, and the journey to get your school where you want it to be sometimes feels insurmountable. By reading to the end of this book, you have already demonstrated that you understand what effective inclusion really means: building a culture where every pupil is seen, valued and given the chance to thrive, sometimes in seemingly impossible situations. The case studies, pedagogy and strategies in this book show that while the challenges can feel daunting, positive change is always possible with persistence, collaboration and the right mindset. Even small, incremental steps taken consistently can transform the experiences of children and young people in your school.

The landscape is shifting around us as this book goes to press. In February 2026, the government published its long-awaited Schools White Paper, *Every Child Achieving and Thriving*, setting out proposals to reform the SEND system in England. The plans include a new layered model of support, with EHCPs reserved for the most complex cases and a new Inclusion Support Plan intended to sit beneath that threshold. A twelve-week consultation was open until May 2026, and the proposals will not become law until they have passed through Parliament. No student will lose support already in place, and the government has confirmed that pupils with EHC plans in mainstream schools will not be moved to any new system before 2030.

While the ambition to simplify the system and improve consistency is welcome, many school leaders and SENDCos are approaching these developments with caution. For years, schools have been expected to meet increasingly complex needs without the funding, staffing or specialist services required to do so effectively. Any reform that places greater emphasis on support within mainstream settings must be matched by meaningful investment in training, capacity and early intervention. Without this, there is a real risk that structural change simply shifts pressure around the system rather than alleviating it.

At the same time, the consultation offers an opportunity for those working closest to children and families to influence what happens next. The voices of school leaders, SENDCos, teachers and parents will be essential in shaping a system that is both realistic for schools to deliver and genuinely responsive to the needs of children and young people. For a detailed review of the White Paper, have a look at the commentary available on my YouTube channel.

I've enormously enjoyed sharing my insights, and I hope they help you build confidently on your school's foundations for inclusion. I always welcome questions from staff in schools, so please do get in touch if you would like to discuss anything further and check back to the companion website for future updates.

Thank you, on behalf of your pupils and their families, for investing in your school's inclusive future.

References

Legislation

Children and Families Act 2014. London: The Stationery Office.

Education and Inspections Act 2006. London: The Stationery Office.

Equality Act 2010. London: The Stationery Office.

L v Clarke and Somerset County Council [1998] ELR 129. Independent Provider of Special Education Advice (IPSEA). Available at: https://www.ipsea.org.uk/l-v-clarke-and-somerset-county-council-1998-elr-129.

Special Educational Needs and Disability Regulations 2014 (SI 2014/1530). Regulation 13. London: The Stationery Office.

Statutory guidance and government publications

Department for Education (DfE) (2014) Special educational needs and disability code of practice: 0 to 25 years. London: Department for Education. Available at: https://www.gov.uk/government/publications/send-code-of-practice-0-to-25

Department for Education (2020) *The Engagement Model*. London: Standards and Testing Agency. Available at: www.gov.uk/government/publications/the-engagement-model

Department for Education (2023) 'What are reasonable adjustments and how do they help disabled pupils at school?', *Education Hub*, 10 April 2023. Available at: https://educationhub.blog.gov.uk/2023/04/what-are-reasonable-adjustments-and-how-do-they-help-disabled-pupils-at-school

Department for Education (2024) *Flexible Working in Schools*. London: DfE. Non-statutory guidance, originally published 24 February 2017; last updated 21 November 2024. Available at: www.gov.uk/government/publications/flexible-working-in-schools

Department for Education (2024) *Working Together to Improve School Attendance: Statutory Guidance for Maintained Schools, Academies,*

Independent Schools and Local Authorities. London: DfE. Statutory from 19 August 2024. Available at: www.gov.uk/government/publications/working-together-to-improve-school-attendance

Department for Education (2026) *Every Child Achieving and Thriving: Schools White Paper*. London: DfE. Published February 2026.

Department for Education and Department of Health (2015) *Special Educational Needs and Disability Code of Practice: 0 to 25 Years*. London: DfE/DoH. Available at: www.gov.uk/government/publications/send-code-of-practice-0-to-25

Ministry of Justice/HMCTS (2023) *Tribunal Statistics Quarterly: July to September 2023*. London: MoJ. Published 14 December 2023. Available at: www.gov.uk/government/statistics/tribunals-statistics-quarterly-july-to-september-2023

Ministry of Justice/HMCTS (2024) *Tribunal Statistics Quarterly: July to September 2024*. London: MoJ. Published 12 December 2024. Available at: www.gov.uk/government/statistics/tribunals-statistics-quarterly-july-to-september-2024

Ministry of Justice/HMCTS (2025) *Tribunal Statistics Quarterly: July to September 2025*. London: MoJ. Published 11 December 2025. Available at: www.gov.uk/government/statistics/tribunals-statistics-quarterly-july-to-september-2025

Ofsted (2025) *Education Inspection Framework: For Use from November 2025*. Manchester: Ofsted. Published 8 September 2025; in use from 10 November 2025. Available at: www.gov.uk/government/publications/education-inspection-framework/education-inspection-framework-for-use-from-november-2025

Ofsted and Care Quality Commission (2025) *Area SEND Inspections: Framework and Handbook*. Manchester/London: Ofsted/CQC. Originally published 29 November 2022; reviewed and updated 7 July 2025. Available at: www.gov.uk/government/publications/area-send-framework-and-handbook

Books and academic sources

Bennathan, M. and Boxall, M. (1998) *The Boxall Profile: A Guide to Effective Intervention in the Education of Pupils with Social, Emotional and Behavioural Difficulties: Handbook for Teachers*. Maidstone: Association of Workers for Children with Emotional and Behavioural Difficulties.

Boddison, A., Curran, H. and Moloney, H. (2021) National SENCO Workforce Survey 2020: Time to Review 2018–2020. Bath: Bath Spa University and nasen.

CAST (2018) *Universal Design for Learning Guidelines Version 2.2*. Wakefield, MA: CAST. Available at: https://udlguidelines.cast.org

Datu, J.A.D., Valdez, J.P.M. and King, R.B. (2022) 'The benefits of kindness: Positive affect mediates the relationship between perceived kindness and student wellbeing', *Journal of Positive Psychology*, 17, (1), 55–66.

Durlak, J.A., Weissberg, R.P., Dymnicki, A.B., Taylor, R.D. and Schellinger, K.B. (2011) 'The impact of enhancing students' social and emotional learning: A meta-analysis of school-based universal interventions', *Child Development*, 82, (1), 405–432.

Gottman, J.M., Katz, L.F. and Hooven, C. (1996) 'Parental meta-emotion philosophy and the emotional life of families: Theoretical models and preliminary data', *Journal of Family Psychology*, 10, (3), 243–268.

Kaplan, D., Miller, S. and Kaplan, E. (2016) 'Evaluation of a kindness education program for first-grade students', *Journal of Moral Education*, 45, (4), 1–16.

Kuypers, L. (2011) *The Zones of Regulation: A Curriculum Designed to Foster Self-Regulation and Emotional Control*. San Jose, CA: Social Thinking Publishing.

Magee, J. (2020) *Kindness Matters: 30 Days That Will Transform Your Life and the Lives of Others*. Blackburn: Kindness Matters.

Reports, frameworks and guidance

British Dyslexia Association (n.d.) *About the BDA*. Bracknell: BDA. Available at: www.bdadyslexia.org.uk/about

Education Endowment Foundation (2020) *Special Educational Needs in Mainstream Schools: Guidance Report*. London: EEF. Published May 2020. Available at: https://educationendowmentfoundation.org.uk/education-evidence/guidance-reports/send

Education Endowment Foundation (2025) *Deployment of Teaching Assistants: Guidance Report*. London: EEF. Published March 2025. Available at: https://educationendowmentfoundation.org.uk/education-evidence/guidance-reports/deployment-of-teaching-assistants

Education Policy Institute (2021) *Identifying Pupils with Special Educational Needs and Disabilities*. London: EPI. Published March 2021. Funded by the Nuffield Foundation. Available at: https://epi.org.uk/publications-and-research/identifying-send

Stiebahl, S. (2025) 'FAQ: ADHD Statistics (England)', House of Commons Library. Available at: https://commonslibrary.parliament.uk/faq-adhd-statistics-england

Johnston, C. and Stanke, C. (2024) *Identifying speech, language and communication needs: Lambeth Early Action Partnership's Evelina SaLT audit and award workforce development service*. London: Lambeth Early Action Partnership (LEAP). Available at: https://leaplambeth.org.uk/reports/upskilling-an-early-education-workforce-and-supporting-communication-development-in-pre-school-children/upskilling-an-early-education-workforce-and-supporting-pre-school-children

Mental Health Foundation (2020) *Kindness Matters Guide*. London: MHF. Available at: www.mentalhealth.org.uk/explore-mental-health/kindness/kindness-matters-guide

Special Needs Jungle (2024) '55% Rise in 2024 SEND Tribunal Appeals. LAs' 1.3% Success Rate Cost £153m. The Cost to Families? Incalculable', *Special Needs Jungle*, December 2024. Available at: www.specialneedsjungle.com/55-rise-2024-send-tribunal-appeals-cost-families-incalculable/

Speech and Language UK (2023) Talk matters: The importance of speech, language and communication to children's futures. London: Speech and Language UK

Key organisations cited

British Dyslexia Association: www.bdadyslexia.org.uk

CAST (Center for Applied Special Technology): www.cast.org

Council for Disabled Children: https://councilfordisabledchildren.org.uk

Education Endowment Foundation: https://educationendowmentfoundation.org.uk

Education Policy Institute: https://epi.org.uk

Nurture UK (Boxall Profile): www.boxallprofile.org

Speech and Language UK (formerly I CAN / The Communication Trust): https://speechandlanguage.org.uk

Companion website

Scan the QR code to access a range of additional resources, including printable materials, templates and further reading.

Index

Other titles by Lynn How:

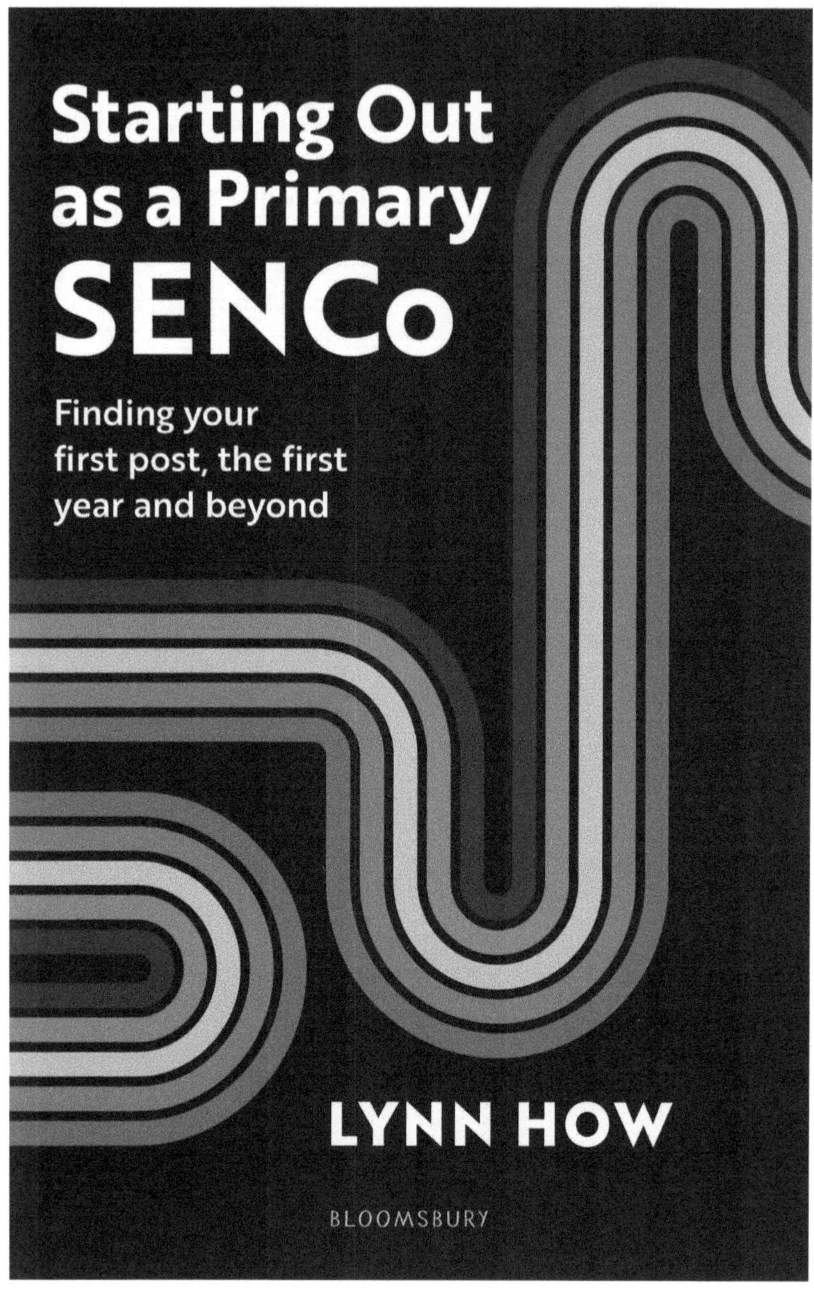